Praise for

CREATE SPECIAL

"*Create Special* is like drinking through the firehose of entrepreneurship. If you want to know what it takes, read this book!"

– John Harthorne, Founder and CEO, MassChallenge

"Jim has helped more businesses than *Yellow Pages* and his passion is infectious. He is a tough-love, take-no-prisoners, not-here-to-be-your-friend kinda guy and this book remains true to this, served up with humility and a keen business mind and presented in a style that everyone can relate to. This is a must-read."

– Bill Morrow, Chairman and Founder, AngelsDen.com

"This book is an easy read and gets you to think a lot about yourself and the way you could change to create something very special. All you have to do is to change your mindset, believe in yourself and things will start to turn around."

– Steven Smith, Founder of Poundland and One Price Shopping

"Over the past five years I've watched Jim Duffy do magical things for entrepreneurs in helping them turn ideas into commercial realities. Through *Create Special* Jim opens up enterprise potential to thousands more, with advice that's succinct and spot-on. I look forward to seeing the impact of this book, with an economy powered by lots more lobsters!"

– Emma Jones, Founder, Enterprise Nation

"Easy-to-read and brimming with useful advice, *Create Special* teaches you everything you need to know to become an entrepreneur. Jim inspires and, most of all, enables ... a must-read for all aspiring entrepreneurs!"

– Ann Gloag OBE, Co-founder of Stagecoach

"Jim has written an inspiring guide for new entrepreneurs, filled with actionable insights, checklists, real-life examples observed close at hand, in his unique down-to-earth voice. Strikingly honest and drawing from hundreds of relationships with top entrepreneurs ... overflowing with tips, questions, new approaches and inspiration, it's an invaluable tool in the entrepreneurial journey."

– Ian Merricks, Chair, The Accelerator Network

"An engaging read – it stands out from the dozens of 'how-to' books out there."

– Abhijeet Bhalla, Co-Founder, Viridian Group

"A must-read, practical, down-to-earth and mindset-changing book. Everything it recommends works in practice and is backed up by experience not psychobabble ... I love the way Jim Duffy is brutally honest about himself, newbie entrepreneurs, peers, celebrity entrepreneurs and, of course, his favourite movies. It's a page-turner!"

– Tony Robinson OBE, 'Freedom from Bosses Forever' Author & Speaker

CREATE SPECIAL

Think & act like an entrepreneur to change your life

JIM DUFFY MBE

Harriman House

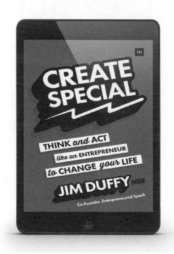

This book is dedicated to the awesome collective who enable people to **CREATE SPECIAL** *in the Entrepreneurial Spark hubs across the UK and India – and especially to Royal Bank of Scotland who are powering a new entrepreneuring revolution.*

HARRIMAN HOUSE LTD

18 College Street

Petersfield

Hampshire

GU31 4AD

GREAT BRITAIN

Tel: +44 (0)1730 233870

Email: enquiries@harriman-house.com

Website: www.harriman-house.com

First published in 2017.

The right of Jim Duffy to be identified as the Author has been asserted in accordance with the Copyright, Designs and Patents Act 1988.

Cover and design copyright © Harriman House

Text copyright © Jim Duffy

Paperback ISBN: 978-0-85719-594-4

eBook ISBN: 978-0-85719-056-7

British Library Cataloguing in Publication Data

A CIP catalogue record for this book can be obtained from the British Library.

Myers–Briggs Types graphic adapted from original by Jake Beech, under Creative Commons license.

CONTENTS

ABOUT THE AUTHOR

Jim Duffy MBE is the co-founder of Entrepreneurial Spark, the world's largest equity-free business accelerator for new-start businesses. Entrepreneurial Spark has 13 hubs in the UK and four in India, from where it enables over 1,000 entrepreneurs annually.

Starting in 2011, Jim built Entrepreneurial Spark from scratch to what has become a phenomenon in enabling early-stage entrepreneurs to **CREATE SPECIAL** by starting and growing new businesses. Jim believes that anyone can learn to be more entrepreneurial through a process of enablement that focuses on mindsets and behaviours. This leads to people becoming credible, backable and investable – in any walk of life.

Jim's work on enabling mindsets attracted big players to back Entrepreneurial Spark across the UK and India, including NatWest, KPMG, Viridian and Dell. He has also been recognised by Ernst & Young for his work with entrepreneurs, and has twice been included in the *Sunday Times* Maserati 100 list of game-changing entrepreneurs.

Jim was made an honorary professor at Glasgow Caledonian University and is a visiting professor at Edinburgh Napier University. He was awarded an MBE in 2017 for his services to entrepreneurship.

Jim lives in Edinburgh and travels extensively, enabling others to create special – and, of course, to think like a lobster.

⚡ **www.create-special.com**

⚡ **@create_special**

INTRODUCTION
Be the Lobster

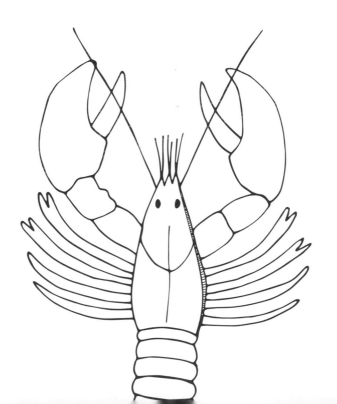

This is not a business book

Hey! How are you? Yes, *you*. So you've picked up, bought or been given this book. You're about to find out how you can change your mindset – and your life.

This whole book is focused on YOU. In fact, I only care about you. It's my blood oath to you from the outset.

This is not going to be a typical business book:

⚡ I am not going to mess around with lots of boring academic theory.

⚡ I am going to shock you.

⚡ I am going to challenge you.

⚡ I am going to get underneath your skin.

⚡ I am going to enable you – while I entertain you.

And I am going to do all of the above – and more – so that I can motivate you to **CREATE SPECIAL**.

I am definitely not going to waste your time. An entrepreneur cannot afford it. I have carefully made this book as concise as possible. I want it to be punchy as hell. I want it to be the sort of book you can read in one day – and reread whenever you need a refresher. I think it's much better to have a book that you can easily get all the way through, and revisit if necessary, rather than a stodgy, long book that you never finish.

Lots of business books are boring. They are filled with strategy this and strategy that. They overflow with diagrams that have been dreamt up on whiteboards. They give you crappy exercises to do while they pontificate on this new theory or that new growth model – all good on paper, perhaps, but it takes no account of YOU.

They're just too sterile, too clinical and prescriptive. And life is just not like that – is it?

Dead already

A few years back I watched a movie called *American Beauty* (1999), directed by Sam Mendes and starring Kevin Spacey, who plays the lead character, Lester Burnham.

Lester is a 42-year-old advertising executive who has lost his spark. Without a purpose in life, events are shaping him, instead of him shaping events. Lester then gets a grip on his life, takes some risks and has some fun along the way. The opening scene is particularly memorable. Lester narrates as the camera works its way through his neighbourhood towards him. It goes something like this:

> "My name is Lester Burnham. This is my neighbourhood. This is my street. This is my house. I'm 42 years old. In less than a year, I'll be dead. Of course, I don't know that yet... And in a way, I'm dead already!"

These words had a powerful effect on me. Imagine going through life feeling dead, being shaped by circumstances, buffeted by other people's actions and then actually dying – having achieved nothing special.

Imagine being dead already...

Apart from being an insanely fabulous movie, *American Beauty* is responsible for me leaving a well-paid job, promotion prospects, pension, savings and security. It was the catalyst for me completely changing my life. It saw me go from being an employee to an employer. From being managed to leading. From being thrown about in other people's waves to making my own waves in my own ocean.

I could say, "Thanks Sam Mendes, you completely screwed up my life!" But, I'd rather shout, "Thanks Sam Mendes – you completely changed my mindset."

Here is my new version of Lester's words as I start Act 3 of my life.

"My name is Jim Duffy. This is my canvas. This is my typewriter (well, I wish... I'm actually working on a Mac). These are my words. I'm 49 years old and in less than a year, I'll be a bestselling author... Of course, I don't know that yet... And in a way, I'm there already."

What will your lines be?

Why you need this book

The world is changing fast. I mean at lightning speed. While writing this book, Donald Trump won the US presidency. Political views aside, the most powerful and respected office in the world is now his. An entrepreneur is sitting in the Oval Office! I didn't see that coming! Did you? The era of the conventional politician is no more.

Turbulent times are ahead. And not just politically. Big corporations that have created and sustained lots of jobs throughout the globe will have to downsize, outsource and deep clean to stay alive and relevant. After all, they have quarterly results to make and shareholders to placate. Many of them are doomed. And jobs for life are no more. Take heed.

Ways of working, living and communicating are also changing like never before. Mobile technology is replicating faster than an amoeba on steroids. Fingerprint access to everything you own and keep secure is on the way. And the tech giants like Google, Amazon and Uber will keep pushing the boundaries as they disrupt – while they fill their balance sheets with reams of cash. It's in their DNA.

Banks will morph from high-street frontages into mobile apps as they re-shape their business models and respond to challenger banks and customers who want to do everything from their smartphones. Big food retailers like Tesco will downsize their huge warehouse-like stores into smaller niche offerings, and old establishment companies like Marks & Spencer will flip from clothing – their traditional staple offering – into food and homeware only. Watch this space!

At the same time as all this, entrepreneurs will invite you to test, sample, buy, play with, share, subscribe to, blog about, win and eat their goods, services and inventions. Others will ask you to invest directly into their companies via equity-based

crowdfunding sites. Traditionally, if you wanted to buy shares in a company you would have to enlist the services of a stockbroker, who would buy and sell shares for you under very strict stock market regulations. But a lot of the bureaucracy or red tape has now disappeared. Indeed, a new start-up 'stock market' is emerging in the form of crowdfunding: you can invest in new entrepreneurial ventures and there's not a stockbroker in sight. Where did that come from?

How we deliver healthcare will change. That's one I'm happy about! I want a pain-free hip replacement when I'm older. How and what we teach our kids will change. That's also a good thing as we are dooming yet another generation to mediocrity in the meantime. In the past few years, religion has also come under the spotlight. For centuries, we were taught to believe in religions like Christianity or Islam or Judaism. But the whole thing has been split wide open. The latest generation does not accept that blind faith is enough. It wants answers. The question of 'Did man create God or did God create man?' has never been so in the limelight. Mind you, there's still a booming business on TV 'God' channels seeking your donations.

There's just a maelstrom of volatility and uncertainty out there. It's all go in this world... And you need to keep up.

A new mindset is needed.

The good news

There's got to be good news, right? Well, I've never been more excited about the huge potential in you and how to bring all of it out. The good news is that you can develop a whole new way of thinking to equip you to either stay ahead of the curve or simply keep up with it and contribute. You can develop new patterns of thinking that lead to gigantic action-taking that will open up a whole new way of doing things to allow you to **CREATE SPECIAL**.

We will look at what creating special is in some depth soon, but for now it's enough to say that it's about creating awesome value for people. From starting a business to growing a business, from coping with change to leading the change, from finding out who you really are to letting others see it and feel it, to making amazing stuff happen in your life and the lives of others – it's a **mindset**.

The mindset of the entrepreneur

Hopefully that's got your juices flowing. Here are some questions to stimulate further thoughts. Based on where you are in your life journey right now:

⚡ Do you really want to think and act like an entrepreneur? Can you be bothered to **CREATE SPECIAL**? Be honest.

⚡ Why is thinking and acting more entrepreneurially important to you?

⚡ What benefits are there of *not* classing yourself as an entrepreneurial thinker?

⚡   What benefits will thinking more like an entrepreneur bring you if you are already on your entrepreneurial journey?

⚡ Have you been conditioned into thinking in mono while there is a big wide world of stereo (and indeed surround-sound) thinking that you have yet to sample?

⚡ Are you up for changing your mindset to optimism and positive-outcome-oriented thinking?

⚡ How do you fancy being a new-age gladiator?

⚡ Where could you be in 12 months or three years if you switch your mindset and behaviours?

⚡ Have you even realised what your own personal relevance is on this earth? Do you know what a *moonshot* is – and can you create one?

It is important for me to get it all out on the table: the development of new and insightful thought processes in your emotionally charged, redundant, neural pathways to help you think more entrepreneurially in life or to sharpen your current entrepreneurial style are the two key focuses of this book.

For me the above questions all boil down to:

How motivated and inspired are you to disrupt your current mindset to achieve something really special?

Do you want to create something special or are you in the throes of doing so? I know so many terrific people in this life and they have so much hidden, untapped potential. They do not believe they can leave a career, create their own job or start a business or an organisation, run a charity, run a marathon or just get out of the rut they are in. They do not believe they can have real impact. In short, they have been conditioned to mediocrity and a lifetime lacking achievement and real fulfilment.

They will never experience, outside children perhaps, the joy of creating something special in the short time they have on this planet. I can change that for you (and with you) – and have changed that for many!

But I need you to become a lobster first.

The lobster in you

Lester Burnham became a lobster. And by reading this book, you will also become a lobster.

I always thought that lobsters were just big shellfish that posh people ate in restaurants. I had no real thought for what it takes to be a lobster – and the true majesty of this particular shellfish.

Lobsters are part of a large family of crustaceans. They have a hard exoskeleton shell. This shell protects them, while also constraining them. In order for a lobster to grow, at various stages of its life it must moult. In other words, it has to get rid of its old shell and start to form a new one.

All sounds pretty simple, right?

Like all things in life that involve growth and change, it's far from simple. For about 20–30 minutes the lobster is vulnerable whilst moulting. It essentially becomes a piece of meat for other aquatic creatures on the prowl. It's a bit like taking all your clothes off and walking into the street.

The lobster faces many threats. It knows this and mitigates as much of the risk as possible – it changes colour and forms additional skin before it moults. However, for the most part Mr Lobster knows that in order to grow larger it simply has to get over the fear of being vulnerable for a while. It has to shed its old shell and get on with it.

In other words, a lobster has to be comfortable being uncomfortable so that it can continue to become a fabulous top-class shellfish.

Just once? No, up to 30 times! *Mr Lobster will moult 25 times in his first five to seven years of existence.* Each time he does this, he wiggles free from his hard and protective exoskeleton, leaving a soft and squishy and very exposed body.

What is more amazing is that, as he moults, he can regenerate lost limbs – even eyes and antennae too. The whole process of being uncomfortable, exposed and defenceless means that Mr Lobster is able to improve himself.

For you to become a top-class shellfish, we need to move you outside your comfort zone. You have to learn from the lobster, so you can improve and grow and be comfortable doing so. You have to try things that you would ordinarily discount as unachievable or not your bag. There's nothing worse than trying something you don't like or that scares you. You feel vulnerable. It's hard work. But by challenging your fears, and being willing to live with a bit of pain, really tremendous things can happen.

At the very least, after reading this book you will never look at a lobster the same way again.

A wonderful thing

The creation of something new and special is a wonderful thing. I truly believe that. It creates value for you and others. This is where the magic happens. It leads to all sorts of interesting stuff! It can lead to:

- wealth
- self-fulfilment
- a sense of purpose
- relevance
- enjoyment.

All the while really stretching you.

If you think you have all the answers and don't really want to be enabled (some super-cocky entrepreneurs I have worked with took that position), then this book is probably not for you. But the cocky entrepreneurs don't make it, guys. They get found out. The savvy ones make it.

If you don't believe in the saying **'Every day is a learning day'** then let's change that. Whether you class yourself as an entrepreneur or an entrepreneurial thinker, or if you simply want to think about becoming more entrepreneurial, is up to you.

Thinking and acting like an entrepreneur can lead to some pretty tremendous outcomes in your life – and, more importantly, the lives of others. I see it day in and day out in our Entrepreneurial Spark (powered by NatWest) hubs. I'm excited for you!

Some personal history

Now we've set the scene, it's time you got to know who is on the other side of the page.

A few years after my original 'Lester Burnham moment', I had a dream that was Entrepreneurial Spark: a business that would enable entrepreneurs in a completely different way. I had been pitching my baby for some time before I got anywhere. Seven long months of research, meetings and coffees. I met with hundreds of people, had lots of interesting conversations, and was made many promises. I got knocked back. I had doors closed in my face. I kissed a lot of frogs.

In the end I raised private investment to build Entrepreneurial Spark as a pretty stereotypical tech-style business accelerator to just get started. In essence, a tech accelerator takes in about 10–15 pretty decent tech-oriented start-ups. The accelerator invests a little capital – say, £20,000. This is essentially beer and pizza money for the start-up teams, while they build and code. The accelerator then helps the start-ups to, well, accelerate in order to get the attention of angel investors. (Angel investors are usually a bunch of folks who have got together in a syndicate. They pool

So why you?

Here are some reasons you might have picked up this book – and how I promise to help you meet your goals.

I want to think and act like an entrepreneur, Jim

If you want to be more entrepreneurial but do not actually have an idea or a business, this book is the ideal tool in helping you get to know and understand you. Yes – that's right – YOU!

This is crucial to you becoming a successful entrepreneur or indeed successful in any walk of life. The old saying, *know thyself*, is as relevant today as it was when some dude coined the phrase in ye olde times. You need to unlearn some of the bullshit in your head. You need to learn new ways of thinking. I do not have a psychology degree, nor do I practise medicine. But I have done 20,000 hours in the world of entrepreneurs. A lot of what you will learn in this book is as practical as it is theoretical in scope, but grounded in real-life thinking and down-and-dirty experience.

I agree with Malcolm Gladwell's theory, explained in the book *Outliers*, that it takes 10,000 hours of practice to become an expert at any given pursuit. Putting that much effort into something with real focus, energy and discipline brings rewards. David Beckham apparently worked so much harder than anyone else before and after team training to develop his skills at free kicks and corners. It worked. He was renowned for the way he could whip a ball into the six-yard box. It made him stand out from the crowd – an outlier. It's all about mindset.

We will come back to David in chapter 5.

As an entrepreneurial thinker you have to focus. That means you need to defrag the hard drive that is your brain. The capacity that this opens up in terms of what you can achieve is staggering. Your ability to act differently will help you navigate start-up, pre-scale and scale-up in a business. Outside of business, it will help you think between the cracks in any given situation. People will stand up and take notice. You will become more outcome-driven. You will have a gladiatorial mindset. You'll learn from every little encounter. And get better every day. You will 'react' to life in a more positive, less disjointed fashion.

You too can become an outlier who leaves a mark on this earth.

I run a business but I don't class myself as an entrepreneur, Jim

If you already run a business and are doing okay – maybe you're self-employed or run a family firm – but do not think of yourself as an entrepreneur, I want to change the way you think to help you become an even bigger success.

After all, you need to skill up to keep alive in the game. You have to be ready for anything.

Thinking and acting like an entrepreneur will set you in good stead for the future. I see many start new ventures that end up plateauing after an initial seed round of investment or when revenues hit a certain level. Things become too hard. The business leaders fail to develop themselves. They don't build a big enough team or attract the right talent.

Thinking and acting like an entrepreneur can help you avoid such burnout in the first place. But if you're already at the end of your tether, it's also the secret of rekindling that spark you possessed when you started off.

You can still change the world.

I am a classic entrepreneur, Jim

If you consider yourself an out-and-out 'entrepreneur' already on the rollercoaster, you need to challenge yourself. I know you. And I know how you think. I know what you're thinking right now. I'm just like you! It is *so* easy to get trapped in the business while forgetting to work *on* the business. But it's never been more important to understand where you are on your journey. You have to flip your thinking: you have to work on the business again.

Thinking and acting like an entrepreneur is the key to this. I will show you how.

I am not an entrepreneur and don't ever plan on being one, Jim

You do not have to be an entrepreneur to benefit from thinking and acting more like one. A lot of the lessons in this book can improve your life even if you don't ever plan to go within a hundred miles of a business plan.

* * *

I hope that's whetted your appetite for what lies ahead. As you can see, there's something here for entrepreneurs of every level of experience. Thinking and acting like an entrepreneur can set you up the right way from the start, reinvigorate you when you've reached burnout, or help you onto even higher levels of achievement when you're already motoring away.

Enough said – it's time to get started and #GoDo!

CHAPTER ONE
The Absolute ESSENCE *of an* Entrepreneur

You are not a dog

f you are going to think and act like an entrepreneur to create special things, then I guess we need to have a good look at the term *entrepreneur*. It has become kind of fashionable to be an entrepreneur. A bit hip, a bit Shoreditch and Silicon Roundabout, a bit tech-oriented, a bit creative industries and digital.

And I must say I've never seen so many guys sporting beards in the start-up world than in the past few years. We also appear to have moved on from jeans and hoodies. There's a lot more style-consciousness about.

But beards are not mandatory. Nor is style-consciousness. Nor is your start-up having anything to do with tech. For the very simple reason that there is no one breed of entrepreneur. An entrepreneur comes in every shape and size. An entrepreneur does not come from stock like a pedigree dog. Entrepreneurs are not created through genealogy or eugenics.

An entrepreneur is formed by experience.

That means you can most definitely develop and flourish as an entrepreneur whoever you are.

In this book, we will go through a process of **entrepreneurial enablement**. I'll go into this deeper in the next chapter, but a key part of it is asking you questions. I'm going to do that now and at intervals throughout the book. Have a really good think about them. It's important to developing your mindset.

When I read a book and some author asks me to think and ponder I usually say, "Yeah, yeah – screw that." I skip and miss half the value of the content. Don't be like me. Apply the questions to you. Take the time to ponder them. Maybe get a notebook or open up your smartphone and jot some thoughts down. Maybe put the book down and go think.

Remember, all this is about you. Every page in here, and everything we're doing, should help you in some way to get a bit better at being an entrepreneur. A key part of this is thinking about the content, applying it to yourself and being honest and vulnerable and uncomfortable. That's how you make progress. And all I care about is you making progress... all the time.

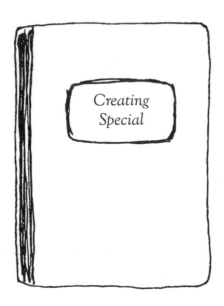

Think and act

⚡ What does the word 'entrepreneur' mean to you?

⚡ Do you class yourself as an entrepreneur? Why?

⚡ Do you know anyone personally or professionally who you would class as an entrepreneur?

⚡ What do you think they look like? Male? Female? Old? Young?

⚡ Do you agree that they have a certain style?

⚡ Do you believe me when I say that you can learn to think and act like an entrepreneur? Why?

Entrepreneurs have no uniform, nor are they uniform in nature. They look like you and me. They bleed when you cut them and they are a fair mix of men and women. They are black, white, gay, straight, religious, non-religious, able-bodied and disabled. Some are mild-mannered, some are hot-tempered. Some like ice cream and some like cookies. They are all individuals. It's what goes on inside their heads that is important. It's all about **mindset.**

I know all shapes and sizes of entrepreneurs but I can't class them into a specific type. What I can say is that I am delighted that the world is producing more and more at all stages of life.

It's a trend – but that's not a bad thing

Lots of people who might not have otherwise done so are now labelling themselves as entrepreneurs. Why is this happening?

Partly I think it's because of the rise of business accelerators, co-working spaces and incubators around the world. You might have heard of names such as Y–Combinator, Techstars and indeed Entrepreneurial Spark. These organisations are designed to help entrepreneurs move faster, while developing those who don't yet class themselves as entrepreneurs into the real deal. It's definitely a hot space to be in.

But it's not the only reason people want to think of themselves as entrepreneurs. A lot of it is because people want to take charge of their destiny.

It's becoming so widespread that I think the next decade is going to be the decade of the entrepreneur.

That's part of the reason this book is able to exist. As an author, I am writing this book with a 'tailwind' behind me. Think of an aeroplane flying at 30,000 feet into a headwind. The plane may be flying at a speed of 500 mph. But the headwind is 50 mph, so it diminishes the progress of the plane. There is increased resistance on the airframe structure. In short, it slows it down.

Now consider the same plane flying at 500 mph with a tailwind of 50 mph. There is no resistance. The plane is pushed along from behind. It has extra oomph.

In the world of books, traditional 'MBA in half an hour'-type tomes are on the wane, while volumes on self-help, turn-your-world-around-in-60-minutes are old hat. Who cares about 25 things that describe an entrepreneur? That doesn't help you think and act like one! It is the entrepreneurial books that inspire *action* that are catching people's eyes. The tailwind behind this book is that teaching business is finished and teaching self-help is not all it's cracked up to be, while mindset is the new black. All the Entrepreneurial Spark enablers who work with early-stage entrepreneurs in our NatWest hubs across the UK focus on this every day.

When you start anything, from a drama group to a charity, a high-growth tech venture to a new food product, make sure you to do not end up fighting against the wind. Find the tailwind and travel with it.

> *Enabler alert:* Creating anything with a tailwind to push it and you along gives a great entrepreneurial boost and can make life easier. Entrepreneurs love a good tailwind and so should you.

Let's dig a bit deeper into 'entrepreneur' to help us understand what it really means to be one.

The practical side

I'm not going to go into a philosophical or academic debate on the word *entrepreneur*. If you Google *entrepreneur* it generates 214,000,000 results in 0.7 seconds. That's a lot of opinion, fact, amazing content and (on occasion) complete bullshit.

There are websites that give you tips each day on how to be successful or how to be a leader or how to write a business plan. There are blogs by guys like Seth Godin. And there are business accelerator websites like Entrepreneurial Spark that aggregate a lot of entrepreneurial thinking and support entrepreneurs in other ways.

In the UK, we have the Centre for Entrepreneurship, which pings out a newsletter every Sunday on what's happening in the world of entrepreneurship that week. We have Enterprise Nation, which again rolls out great content for entrepreneurs and start-ups. We have events all across the country and TEDx talks almost every week, where someone gets up and talks about being an entrepreneur or acting like an entrepreneur or the traits of an entrepreneur that inspire them.

So there's plenty of content available to support you as you read this book. Far be it from me to say I'm the oracle of all knowledge. What we are doing here is considering what is *practically* involved in having an entrepreneurial mindset and what behaviour flows from that – and it is based on my own raw experience of having worked with thousands of entrepreneurs.

Working at close hand with both start-up (early stage) and scale-up (more sophisticated) entrepreneurs and enabling my team of up to 50 staff in Entrepreneurial Spark throughout the UK and India to do the same has given me a thorough insight into what an entrepreneur is and what she is not. And of course I am one of these creatures myself. So that definitely helps.

What is the practical essence of a good entrepreneur, then?

Despite what you might have heard, it is not all about making pots of money. Some of the best entrepreneurs I know and admire are a new breed of entrepreneurs who are changing our neighbourhoods, towns and cities throughout the globe. They are social entrepreneurs.

It annoys me when we worship multi-millionaire entrepreneurs as if they are gods. Sir Richard Branson, Peter Jones or Lord Sugar are successful at what they do – making money. I respect them for their efforts. But for me that is not enough. It does not encapsulate what being an entrepreneur in the 21st century is about. After all, there are thousands of entrepreneurs who put **profit with purpose** ahead of simply amassing great wealth. I kinda like that.

I don't want you to get me wrong – becoming rich out of your work as an entrepreneur is OK! Profit is not a dirty word. If an entrepreneur does not make a profit he will not be in business long. Social or not, the entrepreneur has to have a business model that works.

Additionally, thinking and acting like an entrepreneur is not all about innovation. It's not just creating new inventions in a workshop or lab then bringing them to market. It's not all about exits (selling your company and realising a big pot of cash). Or harvests (realising cash from a business). Or IPOs (listing your company on the stock market).

It's a lot more than these. They are potential outcomes for a hardworking, lucky few. But not the be all and end all.

The essence of a good entrepreneur is great execution on a vision, either for profit or non-profit, that leads to creating something special.

Now let's take some time to consider what you think about this...

Think and act

⚡ What stereotypes do you have in your head of successful entrepreneurs?

⚡ How has the media created – or tainted – the idea of an entrepreneur for you?

⚡ Who are your role models in the world of business? Why?

⚡ Have you been conditioned into thinking that entrepreneurs are just about money?

⚡ Is making pots of cash the right motivation for being an entrepreneur?

⚡ What excites you more: amassing great wealth or doing something socially minded? Or both?

Creating special

When I stand up in front of new start-up entrepreneurs on the first day of their journey in the Entrepreneurial Spark hubs, I ask them:

"Who wants to be a millionaire?"

Usually a scattering of hands go up. I ask:

"Who wants to drive a Bentley Turbo?"

Some of the guys put their hands up.

"Who would like a big house in the country with a housekeeper and some stables?"

A sprinkling of hands pop into the air.

Then I ask the killer question:

"Who wants to create something special?"

It delights me when almost everyone in the room raises a hand with real purpose. A bit like at primary school when the teacher asks the whole class a question and your hand rocketed up as you knew the answer. "Miss! Miss! Miss!"

This is what thinking and acting like an entrepreneur is all about: creating something special. And I love that. Why? Well, let's consider this sucker a bit more...

Special

Special is a word that is underused. When I was a boy, a special delivery was just that. A courier would deliver a pressie and it would generate some excitement in the house (even in the street). But with the likes of Amazon we now get 'special' deliveries coming at us like confetti.

For me, special means exceptional, phenomenal, incredible. These are strong words. Your mum will always say that you are special, even though at times you drove her crazy. Think about what you consider to be special. This will put the word in context. Take a couple of minutes and highlight two special things in your life:

1.

2.

Awesome

Awesome is an American euphemism for 'bloody great!' It's very hip for everything to be 'awesome' in the entrepreneur world. When I visited the MassChallenge start-up accelerator space in Boston, I think I heard "That's awesome!" about 50 times throughout the day.

The Founder and CEO of MassChallenge – John Harthorne – is one of the most positive guys I've ever met. He oozes positivity. He uses the word awesome every ten minutes.

For me, awesome is a great word. It means something that is imbued with the qualities of great, terrific, fabulous, tremendous and wow! I think Porsche is an awesome brand. I think Highland Park is an awesome malt whisky. I believe Muhammad Ali was an awesome individual.

What do you consider awesome? Again, take a couple of minutes and pick two things you feel are awesome:

1.

2.

Value

Value is used in many contexts. But it's safe to say we understand if something represents good value. If I buy a nice bottle of red wine in the supermarket for £6.99, I feel that is good value. It certainly feels good value after the second large glass. However, when I buy the same bottle in a restaurant and it costs me £24, I'm not so convinced.

Primark sells clothes really cheaply on the high street. I wear a casual shirt five or six times in a six-month period. Then it is out of fashion or out of shape. (The shirt – not me.) So, I pay £7.99 at Primark for a shirt that has, say, seven good washes in it before it's done, and I feel I am getting good value for my money.

Awesome and value when put together are pretty powerful. In fact, they're part of the equation that explains special. This is how to think about special as an entrepreneur:

SPECIAL = AWESOME VALUE

If you can create something special, then others will:

⚡ be interested in it

⚡ support it

⚡ buy it

⚡ invest in it

⚡ tell others about it

⚡ work for it

⚡ cherish it

⚡ copy it.

The awesome value you can create as an entrepreneurial thinker is *something people want*. If people – family, friends, potential customers, potential collaborators, suppliers, competitors, investors, politicians, neighbours, club members – perceive awesome value in what you're offering, they will attach themselves to it. And to you.

Awesome value has magnetism. And this is exactly what you want.

Paying for something is just one way that creating something special manifests itself. Steve Smith of

Poundland fame is a great example of that form of awesome value. You just *know* you are getting awesome value there. Steve started on street markets and built an empire based on everything being a pound. No need to have sales. No need to haggle or negotiate or join a loyalty club. Everyone gets one thing and it's communicated effortlessly: awesome value.

But awesome value can be something other than low prices. If you create products or services that people like, want to associate with, engage with, consider relevant or investigate more, then you are onto something. That something is special. It's awesome value. It's what sets great entrepreneurs apart from all the rest, regardless of sector or geography.

Top tips from total lobsters

Business
The Sweet Beet

Sharing new ingredients and flavour pairings in the UK, with a Texas twist.

Owner and founder
Lizzy Hodcroft

Top tips

★ "No one really knows what they are doing. We are just like everyone else and a lot of our success is down to perseverance, timing and luck."

★ "Don't get distracted by 'shiny things'. Focus on what your business needs to grow and stay on track."

★ "Remember your passion and roots. Don't forget where you came from and never ever forget how you got there."

> ★ "The best way to get great and mostly free advertising is if you can find a product that yours complements. Get on the coat tails of those that have a bigger audience reach than you."
>
> ★ "If you don't ask – you don't get!"

It's a lifestyle

You will hear all the usual stuff when the term entrepreneur comes to the fore.

Entrepreneurs are often said to be:

⚡ risk-takers

⚡ business builders

⚡ job creators

⚡ passionate

⚡ determined

⚡ visionaries

⚡ go-getters

⚡ opportunists

⚡ fearless

⚡ persistent.

These are staple descriptors. And they are spot on! There is a lot to each one of them. But to understand the mindset of an entrepreneur you need more than just words in a big list. I guess the best definition that I can give you to really help you get to grips with becoming an entrepreneurial thinker and actor is this:

*An entrepreneur lives a few years of her life, like most people will not –
so that she can spend the rest of her life, like most people cannot.*

An entrepreneur will make sacrifices for a period to achieve
something great – with awesome value – that hopefully at the
end of it all will result in a gain.

Enabler alert: A key entrepreneurial mindset is being
ALL IN for a purpose.

The gain can be financial. It could be job creation. It could be
making a positive impact on society, getting recognition for your
work, or simply satisfaction. The point to note is that it takes
time. Hours, days and months.

**There are no shortcuts to becoming a millionaire or sorting
out a problem in society.**

If you want to be a millionaire, buy a lottery ticket and pray. Every
seasoned entrepreneur you will ever speak to will tell you that it
took them a hell of a lot longer then they originally thought to
get where they wanted to be. Entrepreneurs are **optimists** who
believe they can change the world in jig time. It is only when one
gets immersed in fixing a problem or building a business that the
medium- and long-term realities become apparent.

But that still won't ultimately stop an entrepreneur.

Enabler alert: An entrepreneur does not think about
the glass being half empty or half full – she thinks
about how to refill it.

Think and act

⚡ Where is your headspace right now? Is it ready and willing to develop a new set of skills?

⚡ How optimistic would you say you are?

⚡ Are you committed to months or years of hard graft and sacrifice in order to do something special?

⚡ How does being all in make you feel?

⚡ Do you believe you can do something so much better than it is already being done?

No CV required

Many people work 9–5 for a paycheque. They wake up, get ready and go out to work. They have a boss, colleagues and a role to play. Some work on a minimum wage, some get the living wage, others have a decent hourly rate or annual salary. The job offers benefits: a pension or a company car or a laptop. There is a minimum statutory holiday entitlement. And sick pay. If you are lucky there is a career path and a ladder you can climb. Usually, as you progress up the ladder, the pay rises. This acts as an incentive to stay at the company, while allowing you to climb the social ladder outside work.

I would argue that a 9–5 job acts as an inhibitor. It chains you to a millstone and curtails your true potential. If you're an entrepreneur, it is death.

An entrepreneurial lifestyle is the complete opposite of this. You break free of drudgery. You think ahead. At times others simply cannot keep up with you. You constantly want to fix things. People. Stuff. Systems. Processes. In short, you want to make things happen differently. You approach things from a different angle.

> *Enabler alert:* An entrepreneur creates stuff that is demonstrably different. Have you or can you do the same?

As a result of this the entrepreneur does not see his life's work as CV building – rather it is all about **skilling up**. It becomes a lifestyle. It's grounded in thinking and acting in short bursts over a long period to achieve a vision.

> *Enabler alert:* An entrepreneurial mindset means being on a constant journey of skilling up...

Entrepreneurs think differently. We just do. We see things from a different perspective. We look at the world through a different lens. We are not necessarily any cleverer or smarter than anyone else. You don't have to have been the brainy kid at school. In fact, you might have been a disruptive influence.

I recall my primary five teacher shouting to me across the classroom one wet Wednesday afternoon:

"Jim Duffy, you are the instigator of all the trouble in this class!"

At the time I felt she was being dramatic. After all, I had only split open another boy's head with my ruler during a rained-off playtime. But upon reflection she might have had a point.

The key thing to grasp is that **entrepreneurs are just ordinary people capable of doing extraordinary things with great focus.**

That sounds a bit bumptious. But it's a fact. And one you are hopefully now beginning to embrace. It's good news – because while some people are born entrepreneurs, everyone has it in them to become one. As my old Babson prof used to say when asked whether one is born or made an entrepreneur, "I don't give a crap, Duffy!" Anyone can think and act more entrepreneurially.

Top tips from total lobsters

Business
Desk Dragons

VR video game developers.

Managing director
Benjamin Mills

Top tips
★ "Look at your valuation. You should work it out with external help or it will come back to bite you later."

★ "It isn't all great times and amazing dreams – you will be making sacrifices in all aspects of your life. Of course, the rewards are also personal."

★ "Make sure your first hires are the right people, so give them a rigorous interview process. Your early employees can be the difference between sinking and swimming."

★ "Be agile."

Dispelling the myths

The media can make the world of the entrepreneur look scary at times. I want to dispel the myth of the media or TV entrepreneur. Programmes like *Dragons' Den*, *Shark Tank* and *The Apprentice* present a jaundiced view of what thinking and acting like an entrepreneur is all about. I can't bring myself to watch them anymore.

You have to remember that programmes like that are all about creating drama. Their aim is (understandably) to be good TV. Not to be useful for entrepreneurs.

But as entrepreneurs we look for opportunities in all things. And there are two or three important lessons we can take away from these programmes.

1. Control issues

The first thing these programmes teach us is to **beware others' control**.

You'll have seen what happens when entrepreneurs end up trying to negotiate control of their ventures in, for instance, the *Den*. The entrepreneur is often desperate. The Dragon can take it or leave it. It is no surprise that the deals that get hammered out massively favour the latter.

The minute you get dictated to by someone else in a position of power – financial or otherwise – you are in big trouble. I have found that out to my cost. It can become a source of great stress in your life.

You have to understand the psyche of the Dragons – or those in a similar position. They want to win, own, control and direct. That is why they ask for huge chunks of equity for measly sums of money. Their goal is to be in the driving seat. To get their talons deep inside your enterprise.

Entrepreneurial thinkers never let this happen. They always have escape routes. They create competitive tension elsewhere so that they aren't cornered.

> *Enabler alert:* **An entrepreneurial thinker always has three opportunity tunnels ready for use.**

In *The Great Escape* (1963), Allied POWs plan how to break out of a German prison camp. The Escape Committee decides to dig three tunnels. They name them Tom, Dick and Harry. Why three? If any of the tunnels collapse or are discovered while being dug, the POWs can fall back on the other two. It soon proves a brilliant strategy, as tunnel 'Tom' is discovered. Tunnel 'Harry' goes on to become the stuff of legend. On the night of 24 March 1944, the prisoners get together in Hut 104 and crawl along the 100 feet of this tunnel – and escape the camp. (What happens next isn't quite according to plan, of course, but the principle of having a back-up is still sound!)

You need to adopt this thinking as an entrepreneur. An entrepreneurial thinker has three outcomes in her head at any one time and is ready to seize whichever turns out to be the most workable, opportune or durable.

2. They want to work with people they like to work with

These media entrepreneur programmes also shine a helpful light on the type of people who have been uber successful and how they think and act.

What do we see?

They take no prisoners. They tolerate no flummery. They have a nous for commerciality and a short attention span. But the biggest attribute – and one you must acquire too – is that they want to work with people they believe they will like working with.

The Dragons will always pick a person or team they believe fits their mould. Lord Sugar always goes with the candidate he feels can work best with him. This is vital. As you develop ideas for stuff that you want to do and pitch them to people, remember that business models do not build businesses – people do.

Take heed from the TV entrepreneurs and make sure that, wherever you are, you give an accurate, honest and authentic account of yourself. And look for the same in others you hire or work with. There is nothing more powerful than creating your own tribe.

Enabler alert: **A great entrepreneur will fill the gaps in his plan by enlisting others to the cause.**

3. They are ruthless

These TV entrepreneurs also invariably have a ruthless streak. You'll need one of those too while we're at it. That sounds a bit harsh but it's true. Ruthless does not mean callous or evil. It does not mean being out to do anyone a bad turn. These entrepreneurs are just out to win from every deal. You need to be as well.

Think and act

⚡ Are you mentally equipped to get the best deal in all situations?

⚡ Does negotiation scare you?

⚡ How ruthless are you prepared to be to win? Do you like winning?

⚡ Have you got what it takes to cut through bullshit?

⚡ And get a deal/decision/outcome over the line?

⚡ Can you read people?

Entrepreneurs don't like being told what to do

Whether you are 'naturally' entrepreneurial or it hits you later on in life, it makes no real difference. It took me until I was 35 before I decided to become my own boss. The average age of the entrepreneurs in the Entrepreneurial Spark spaces is 37. Being an entrepreneur is not the 21-year-old stereotype people often think it is.

I was a police officer in Scotland. "Boo hiss!" I hear you say. Relax – I wasn't a traffic cop. I was a real cop. And based on my primary school teacher's comments, it was obvious I should have never become one. Nonetheless, I ended up pounding the beat in the

East End of Glasgow as PC Shiny Buttons in some pretty tough places.

I was always arguing or a bit prickly with those who managed me. In a disciplined organisation like the police, you are supposed to do what you're told. Asking hard questions of 'gaffers' is frowned upon. Mainly because most of them were thick. I was identified early as one to watch or a 'good prospect' and I would have been promoted earlier if it had not been for my prickly demeanour when being told what to do (or my over-ambitious desire to get up the ladder – AKA just move a bit faster). Hence, when I did get promoted to sergeant with only nine years' service – pretty quick in those days – I was still not happy.

Then I had an epiphany. I worked out that I would not be chief constable for another 20 years. I had another five ranks to progress through, with at least two different roles in each rank. Which meant I had to take orders until then.

So I quit.

And I became the chief constable of my own business the next day. Yippee! Boy, did I feel free! I was now starting my own entrepreneurial journey, albeit I had no clue as to what that looked like.

Enabler alert: **An entrepreneur will strip out all the resistance to having control in the early days.**

Think and act

⚡ Have you been conditioned into being managed? Are you happy to play it safe?

⚡ How do you feel about authority?

⚡ Is your boss or the job you are in actually holding you back from why you were put on this planet?

⚡ Do you like being told what to do?

⚡ How can you test your own ability to lead or take control more?

So becoming an entrepreneur can take place at any stage in your life. You might have already begun. Or you might just be thinking about it.

The early stages of an entrepreneur

I've worked with hundreds of early-stage entrepreneurs of all shapes and sizes in our amazing entrepreneurial hubs at NatWest. When I refer to early-stage entrepreneurs, I mean those starting up or pre-scaling a business. That means folks with an idea right up to those with £5 million turnover or £5 million in investment.

There are arguments all over the world as to when an entrepreneur is 'early stage'. My old Babson College professor told me that he referred to early-stage entrepreneurs at $70 million. And I get that. There are investment hot spots across the globe. But, hey ho, it might be a bit arguable, but in the UK we are talking about up to £5 million.

This is a fairly large number! To get a business to £5 million in revenue or bring in £5 million in private investment or debt finance is not easy. It takes a shed load of work. But it's such a fun place to be! It's a time when a business is particularly vibrant, edgy and full of character... and a time when you can make great gains at pace. This stage in a business's life is when entrepreneurs learn so much about what it actually means to be an entrepreneur.

I've seen people build great ideas and businesses from scratch. I've watched in awe as ideas we have discussed on a whiteboard became real businesses, generating revenues, employing people and attracting investment. I've seen small acorns become large trees.

I have also seen people ruin great ideas and businesses. I've seen people implode as they embark on business building for the wrong reasons or with a head full of faulty wiring. It's not pretty. It can be costly – both on a financial level and on a human level.

I've worked with hugely successful entrepreneurs who have brought in big investments and exited for millions. And I am convinced that the same patterns of thinking and acting were threaded through everything they do. And they often developed and perfected those patterns in the early stages of their companies' lives.

What kind of an entrepreneur is in you?

As I've said, entrepreneurs are not all driven by money. We do not all want to become filthy rich. We do not all want private jets. We do not all want to own our own islands. As I wrote this book, Sir Philip Green, the boss of Arcadia, who is worth billions of pounds, was undergoing real scrutiny. He and his wife had just bought another multi-million pound yacht. He lives in Monaco. His business dealings came under the spotlight as a result of the unexpected closure of BHS, a firm he sold in 2015 for £1, and the ramifications (not good) this had for BHS pensions. The House of Commons decided he was no longer fit to retain his knighthood.

For me, Mr Green represents the unacceptable face of entrepreneurship: the **toxic entrepreneur.** Many such entrepreneurs have amassed great wealth – billions. Perhaps that's too much for one individual on this planet to own. But we are where we are. You can be part of a better definition of entrepreneur as you read and act on this book. I'm counting on you...

My words of caution are: money is a byproduct of being a great entrepreneur in whatever field or sector you operate within. Be careful that it never consumes you. Set out to **CREATE SPECIAL**. Don't set out with a crass figure on exit in mind and the make of yacht you are going to buy emblazoned on your forehead.

You will be a lot happier. You will actually enjoy the journey.

Top tips from total lobsters

Business
Fatburn Extreme
Training instructors in the best way to burn fat.

CEO
Dianne Teo

Top tips

★ "There will be peaks and troughs, be prepared to get comfortable with being uncomfortable."

★ "Know your customers – without them you won't have a business."

★ "Know your numbers – as soon as you realise how you can scale your numbers and build your business, it suddenly becomes a reality. A pleasant one!"

The entrepreneurial secret sauce

There is no magic potion needed to think and act like an entrepreneur. No dark arts. No black magic. No voodoo.

There is no science to it, either, though professors of entrepreneurship in universities will say there is. (How else would they justify their existence?)

Unfortunately, though, you cannot just buy a book on entrepreneurship and become a great entrepreneur. If it was that easy, we'd all be millionaires already. What you are doing here is learning the fundamentals of 'applied' entrepreneurship:

in essence, the practical ways seasoned entrepreneurs approach problems and indeed their lives.

I prefer to use the term **Entrepreneuring®** to describe this.

For me, entrepreneurship is a subject studied and taught at universities. It has theoretical connotations. Whereas, entrepreneuring (a term that I have trademarked) is more about the pragmatics of being an entrepreneur. There is a huge gap in studying business and actually taking action and executing. I would not hire 90% of folks with an MBA. Why? Simply put, they cannot execute for toffee.

As Gordon Gekko says in the movie *Wall Street* (1987), "Most of these Harvard MBA types don't add up to dog shit. Give me guys that are poor, smart and hungry."

Smart being the operative word here... Entrepreneurs are smart, not necessarily the brightest academically.

Conclusion

In summary, then, the term entrepreneur can mean different things. But the term is not important: *you* are. What you want to achieve and how you want to get there is key. Money is a byproduct of creating something special. A willingness to put in long hours, make sacrifices and go the extra mile is what it takes to **CREATE SPECIAL**. You have to be your own boss – in your own headspace, accountable and responsible for your own destiny and decisions. You must be willing to be ruthless in decision-making to win through. You must possess willingness to skill up and not remain too comfortable where you are. And you must treat every day as a learning day.

The rest of the book will show you how to do all of this.

Whatever your circumstances, you have the opportunity and the potential to **CREATE SPECIAL**. No qualifications necessary. No sartorial requirements. No family bloodline that says you have a right to think and act entrepreneurially. No need to focus on moneyed role models. No CV required. All it takes is you and a willingness to be a lobster.

In the next chapter we'll explore the first stage of changing your life by thinking and acting like an entrepreneur: it's all about being enabled.

CHAPTER TWO
How to be ENABLED

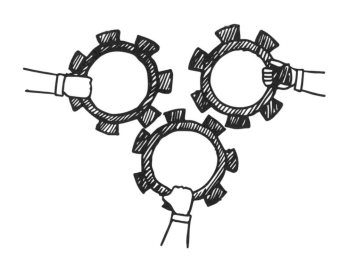

Consultant or enabler?

There are a multitude of people and organisations out there that can educate you, coach you, consult with you, mentor you and advise you. Some are very good at what they do. Some are not. It is important to understand the difference. It will help you frame what enablement is: because by the end of this book you will become your own enabler... and put me out of business.

An educator will act differently from, say, a coach. A consultant will operate differently from a mentor. Each has its own place on your journey. You will meet them and engage with them, employ them, learn from them. As an entrepreneurial thinker, you must be fully aware of their motives and skill sets.

All of them have something to contribute. But the most important thing is to find yourself an entrepreneurial enabler – either an individual or a group of people each contributing something to your journey. That's because ultimately entrepreneurial enablement involves a bit of:

⚡ education

⚡ coaching

⚡ consulting

⚡ mentoring

⚡ and advice.

That's because there are:

⚡ things you don't know (but can learn)

⚡ things you'll need to (and can) get better at

⚡ things you'll need feedback on

⚡ things other entrepreneurs have experienced before (and can show you how to navigate)

⚡ things you will have to rely on outsiders for (you can't do everything yourself).

One of the above is a bit different to the others. Something of an industry has grown up around **consulting**. And it can be very tempting to give consultants too much of a role or a say in your business. Their help is tailored just for you, after all. But ultimately it's the opposite of enablement – you aren't empowered; you're just reliant on the consultant. And there's arguably a financial incentive for consultants to not actually be that helpful at all in the long run.

Consider a patient going to see her doctor. In the UK, top doctors in our hospitals are actually called consultants. They have gone through tough training and long shifts over many years to earn that title. As the patient sits there, the consultant asks her lots of questions. He is trying to diagnose what is wrong. He may ask for some lab tests to help him in this task. Either way, a diagnosis leads to a treatment and care plan. The social contract between doctor and patient is sacred; the doctor has taken a Hippocratic oath and his whole vocation is to help each patient the best he can. He builds his reputation and that of his hospital upon it.

Compare this with a business consultant. You are sitting in front of Mr Business Consultant. Just like the medical consultant, he will ask you questions in an attempt to understand the issues in your business. However, once he has done so it is not in his interests to fix you and be done with it. Far from it. It is the remit of the business consultant to string out his diagnosis. Why? Well, he is probably on a day rate and the more days he spends 'fixing' you, the more cash he generates. At the very least, he is not incentivised to clear everything up as quickly or as cleanly as possible. Better by far if you still need him six weeks, six months, six years from now...

Many an entrepreneur has been stung here (including myself). Please be careful. It can be costly. Especially as you start on your entrepreneurial journey. It's a big generalisation, I know, and if you are a business consultant reading this you may be fizzing mad. Tough!

---

from total lobsters

Business
Foodinate

A social enterprise teaming up with restaurants so that every Foodinate-branded meal enjoyed in a restaurant results in a meal for a local person in need.

CEO and founder
Caroline Stevenson

Top tips
★ "Just go for it – if you don't you'll never know and always regret it."

> ★ "Surround yourself with support – one thing that's not talked about enough is how isolating entrepreneurship can be."
>
> ★ "Don't be afraid to ask – and never forget to say thank you!"

An enabler

As said, an *enabler* is a bit of a combination of each of the people above, including consultant – just without the financial sting in the tail.

Treat this book as YOUR enabler!

After all, I am writing this book to:

⚡ **educate you** by teaching you what it takes to be a successful entrepreneur, revealing all the practical nuts and bolts of how do to it

⚡ **coach you** to think and act more entrepreneurially, developing and refining your mindset and behaviour in ways that really matter

⚡ **consult with you** by asking you questions along the way and showing you how to use your answers to drive yourself and your business ahead

⚡ **mentor you** by sharing from my own personal experience as an entrepreneur, as well as the experience of loads of other entrepreneurs with whom I have worked closely over the years

⚡ **advise you** by revealing all the advice I wish I had been given when I was starting out.

In short, entrepreneurial enablement is a cognitive process that steers you – but also asks you to think hard about yourself and your business. It does not provide generic answers. It holds you accountable for a whole host of metrics – tangible actions and intangible mindset shifts. **YOU make the decisions.**

And ultimately this is all so empowering that *you* become your own enabler.

Think and act

⚡ Do you understand the difference between a consultant and an enabler?

⚡ Do you understand the consulting model of business?

⚡ Write down what you think enablement feels and looks like for you.

⚡ Why do you think an enabler is more relevant to you right now?

⚡ Can you see and feel how you can become your own enabler?

As part of the enablement process that entrepreneurs go through in the Entrepreneurial Spark hubs, each is allocated an enabler. It is her job to hold the entrepreneur to account. The entrepreneurs love this! It forces them to think differently and to be truly honest with themselves. After all, the stakes are high. No one will pay them a wage at the end of the month.

> *Enabler alert:* Entrepreneurs don't blame or moan – they know the buck stops firmly with them.

Enablement holds you to account for your action or lack of it. Let me give you an example.

Enablement in action

A young man comes into the Entrepreneurial Spark hatchery with an idea. He has no real clue about business. But inspiration has struck. He joins the programme and gets started.

His idea is to go to big clothing retailers who have stores in shopping malls. He will do a deal with them to install beacons on their premises. These beacons will send and receive wireless signals to and from each other and to and from customers with smartphones. The young man wants to sign up customers to an app that connects to this beacon network. When a customer with that app installed on his phone walks past one of the stores in the mall, a beacon will ping the customer a deal. For example, it may read:

> *"Hi Jim – we have a sale on today for you only. Get your favourite jeans and we will give you 50% off a new leather belt to go with them."*

As a customer, I then respond or not. It brings me into the shop or not. But all the time it is generating data on how I move about the mall and my buying patterns in shops.

This young lad pitched this idea at Entrepreneurial Spark. As his enabler, I knew that it would take months of work and pots of cash to ever get it off the ground. But it's not my job to stifle creativity and energy. Or to kill someone's dream – even if it is chimerical. So as part of the enablement process I sent him to validate his idea with some local malls. He did. He went out bursting with enthusiasm...

For the next 12 weeks, it all went quiet.

I met him a few times at scheduled Temperature Checks (part of the Entrepreneurial Spark programme). He had lost focus and appetite for the idea. Before long he knew it was not a goer. He had discovered it for himself. And by enabling him to come to that realisation, he could live with it – and move onto new ideas – rather than feeling held back.

I challenged him to find something else that got his juices going. He did. In fact, he's doing great in his new venture, having raised £2 million and with nearly 10,000 customers on his books.

So entrepreneurial enablement is not there to tell you what to do – or to tell you what you want to hear. Nor is it there to do the work for you. It guides and steers those who want to **CREATE SPECIAL**, by helping them see things clearly within an action-oriented framework. It holds you accountable for how you go about things – without getting in the way.

Re-imagine, GoDo, Re-shape

People like to have a saying or a slogan to help them remember and act on stuff. I wanted to boil down entrepreneurial enablement to something really simple. So on a Sunday afternoon in the Glasgow hatchery, I set about crafting what it was all about. And here it is:

Re-imagine, GoDo, Re-shape

These three things get to the crux of it. When you're enabled by this book – and by yourself as you build experience over time – it's these three actions that you'll be performing again and again. Let's explore them.

Re-imagine

Life will present you with problems. As I write this book, I have many problems in my private and professional lives. In fact, this morning I wrote down my immediate problems in a notebook. They are not problems that are insurmountable. Nevertheless, I have to deal with them.

The language I use in my head is important. I can refer to these as *problems*. Or I can refer to them as *challenges*. Or I can refer to them as *issues*. Or I can refer to them as *troubles*. I can let them tax me as I worry about them or I can see them as a way to stretch me or inspire me. One thing is for sure, I cannot let them down me.

The best way for me to enable myself to solve them is to **re-imagine** them.

By reimagining a set of circumstances, a whole new perspective is opened up. Problems are reframed and redefined – and a wide range of solutions present themselves. Some of you are natural worriers. A problem will whizz around your head for hours until it exhausts you. Many of us worry about a problem and get tired as a result of the worrying – and then the problem seems even bigger. It's a vicious cycle. And reimagining a problem breaks it.

Let's try something. Take a problem or challenge in your life right now. Get a piece of blank paper or a new page in your notebook. Put the problem in the middle of the page – like this:

Now draw off branches from the problem that look at it from different perspectives. There could be your initial perspective, the perspective of a loved one, a colleague, your boss, a friend, an organisation. Ask yourself questions about the size of the problem or challenge. Consider timescales and deadlines. Ask yourself a bunch of 'what if?' questions around it. Give the problem to someone else and imagine it is theirs and you have to solve it for them. Think up a few scenarios where it becomes *less* of a challenge – and a few where it becomes *more* of a challenge. Imagine yourself six months from now. How does the problem look? What do you think could have influenced it, reduced it or made it bigger? Which people are involved in this problem? Who else should be – or should not?

You will see that you are reframing the problem or challenge into something else. You are playing with it to structure it differently. You are taking the emotion out of it. You are considering circumstances that could come into play. By reimagining the problem, you start to open up new possibilities and potential.

You bring in light at the end of the tunnel.

GoDo

Now that you have thought about a problem or challenge from a few different perspectives and re-imagined it, you will have unearthed some opportunity tunnels. Remember, ideally you want three of these – you pursue the best but can fall back on the other two if you need to. Then it's time to take action. It's time to explore some of these opportunities. It's time to **GoDo**.

As an entrepreneur, you will soon understand the need to focus and work even when you feel uncomfortable. You can't always be inspired. You won't always be self-confident. But you cannot let that hold you back. Remember, entrepreneurs are made as well as born. Having a GoDo mindset gets you past these moments. After a while, it even functions without having to think too hard about it. And when your default setting is **GoDo**, you are truly cooking with gas.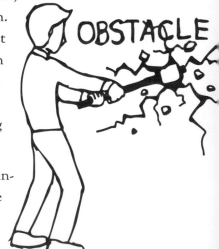

We've all heard the term 'can do'. A can-do attitude suggests someone positive about her ability to be successful at something. But it does not mean she will. It's too reactive (instead of proactive) for my tastes. When I go to the gym, for instance, I *can* do some deadlifting. Whether I will or not is entirely down to whether I feel like it! And that's no good when you want results.

Hence I prefer **GoDo**.

These two words are designed to result in action. You have to go and do. There are no ifs, buts or maybes implied. It's a make-it-happen, action-oriented phrase that is burned into the psyche of every successful entrepreneur.

Entrepreneurs are all about taking action – constantly.

Think and act

⚡ Think of a time when you just did not GoDo. What stopped you from doing so?

⚡ How prepared are you to make sacrifices in order to GoDo?

⚡ Could you make GoDo your default setting?

⚡ How will you know when you have switched to a GoDo mindset?

When writing this book, I wanted every mention of **GoDo** to be #GoDo. There's a good reason for this – though, in the interests of keeping the text as readable as possible, we've stuck with plain old 'GoDo' for most of the text.

If you haven't already, have a look on Twitter at the hashtag #GoDo. (Type '#GoDo' into the search bar on your app or at **www.twitter.com**.) It is one of the most positive hashtags on Twitter. (A hashtag, if you didn't know, basically links a tweet that includes it with every other tweet that has ever used it. Clicking on the hashtag in one tweet brings up every tweet it's appeared in. It's a way of easily reading or contributing to a conversation.)

The #GoDo hashtag is of course linked to the @ESparkGlobal tweets (and my tweets at @create_special) and together they form an important part of Entrepreneurial Spark's online presence. This is why I try to never refer to #GoDo without giving it a hashtag symbol. It's a way of life!

Have a look at the hashtag now; see the conversations going on – there'll be lots of examples of going and doing to take inspiration from.

Think and act

⚡ Get on Twitter…now!

⚡ Follow the following people:

  ⚡ @create_special

  ⚡ @ESparkGlobal

   ⚡ #GoDo

  ⚡ #createspecial

⚡ Now, give them a tweet… :)

⚡ Can you feel the positivity around the hashtag?

In developing a GoDo mindset, there are a number of things we need to take into consideration. I need you to think about them collectively. The mindsets and behaviours we will discuss do not act in isolation. Imagine it this way…

I love watching aeroplanes take off. The power of the Rolls-Royce or GE engines on a Boeing 777 is remarkable. Up they go to 30,000 feet. At this altitude, they are cruising. It looks effortless. The aeroplane floats across the sky, the captain sticks on autopilot… But a multitude of operations are going on here:

⚡ the engines are pumping out thrust to provide sufficient speed over the wings

⚡ the ailerons are moving quickly to react to any sudden air movements to keep the plane steady

⚡ the rudder is pitched in such a way to keep everything smooth

⚡ the radar is sweeping ahead to check for weather systems

⚡ the engines are charging the batteries to keep the heating on to keep the passengers warm and cook the food

⚡ the computer is working out fuel consumption, navigation and keeping everything on an even keel.

This is called **trim**. As you sit in your seat, drinking your gin and tonic and watching your inflight movie, all of this is taking place around you. But you are not aware of it. And this is what a GoDo mindset looks like. Your thought processes are in trim. You are taking action hour to hour, day to day, week to week. And everything is in sync to help you take that action. The mindset and behaviours we will discuss are all acting in concert to help you get to where you want to be.

Top tips from total lobsters

Business
Whisky Frames
Creating rustic picture frames out of of old whisky barrels.

Owner
Kristen Hunter

Top tips
★ "Learn quickly. Try things. And don't give up. It is all about decisiveness, and adapting and developing quickly."

Re-shape

Having taken positive action to address your re-imagined problem, now you have to re-shape. This is all about learning for the long term. It sets you in great stead. It makes obstacles easier to overcome. It makes you bolder and stronger – and keeps you moving forward. Ask yourself:

⚡ What did I **learn** having taken action on my re-imagined problem?

⚡ What **surprised** me that I maybe took for granted?

⚡ What **assumptions** did I get wrong?

⚡ Was the **timing** of the problem way out of kilter?

⚡ Was my **understanding** of what other people thought about it right or wrong?

⚡ What can I do now to **resolve** it to a better conclusion?

⚡ Was it worth causing me so much **worry**?

Be a better version of you

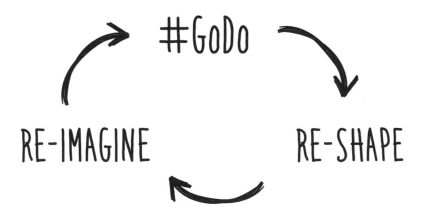

#GoDo

RE-IMAGINE   RE-SHAPE

Case study: Re-imagine, #GoDo, Re-shape

Business name / Name of entrepreneur
Orbit Enterprise Education / Kieran Aitken

Business proposition / What does it do? / How does it do it?

A teenage Business Incubator: "On a mission to inspire the next generation to think bigger". Orbit is an inspiring and practical ten-week programme to support teenagers who have an interest in entrepreneurship. With the support of RBS and a network of dedicated mentors, Orbit takes 60 young people aged 16–18 and supports them to set up, launch and run their own businesses. With access to workshops and senior business leaders and experts, Orbiteers will build outstanding commerciality skills, make money and boost their CVs.

How has the entrepreneur changed how he thinks and acts in order to create special?

Kieran joined Entrepreneurial Spark aged 18 and fresh out of high school. After dabbling in entrepreneurship with a small car-washing business and an insatiable appetite for all commerce books, Kieran came into the programme with a desire to share his fascination of entrepreneurship with other young people.

Surrounded by older and what he considered 'wiser' entrepreneurs, Kieran adopted a tough and businesslike demeanour to fit in. This had the unintended effect of coming across as over-confident and cocky. The very passion and charm of youth, which underpins his entire proposition, was diluted – with Kieran trying to replicate the men in stuffy suits he had so looked up to.

Kieran, with the help of his enabler, got straight out of his comfort zone, took a crash course in self-awareness and after some challenging conversations underwent a radical transformation. He remained confident but quietly so, retained his business savviness but was happy to admit he didn't know it all. He reintroduced that refreshing quality that is so evident in 18-year-olds who want to go forward and take over the world.

Kieran's business has grown from strength to strength since joining the programme, but more impressively, he has grown hugely as a leader. Always the first to volunteer to pitch, always helping his fellow entrepreneurs and always turning information learned in Entrepreneurial Spark into action.

Another early challenge – and breakthrough – came after two successful programme intakes in Glasgow. It was soon evident to Kieran that to grow Orbit and reach his bold vision of being the largest social enterprise for teenagers in the UK, he'd need more than just himself and a few volunteer helpers. His business is heavily reliant on him – he engages with the schools, he recruits the mentors and he facilitates the programme – and while he's able to manage this independently when the programme is close to home, this is not sustainable for major UK cities.

As a result Kieran has had to focus on reimagining his business model for growth. With limited start-up funds, he understands that building relevant networks and securing key partners to share and assist with resourcing his business is absolutely crucial to Orbit's success.

Kieran is very much 'eye on the prize' and when he has a goal in sight, displays true tenacity and #GoDo spirit until that goal is realised. He had targeted large corporations with nationwide presence – and it's no easy feat for a small Scotland-based start-up to get an audience with them. Despite limited response to his constant phone calls and emails, Kieran continues to be relentless (and increasingly creative) in pursuit of his goal.

Orbit has now secured a partnership with one of the UK's

largest banks, which will provide physical premises for him throughout the UK, and is in discussion with one of the largest youth charities in the UK, which will help him access its staff, mentor pool and more. This will allow Kieran to take his business to the next level and launch in a city near you soon.

Case study: Re-imagine, #GoDo, Re-shape

Business name / Name of entrepreneur
Friction Free Shaving / Aidan Burley

Business Proposition / What does it do? / How does it do it?
FFS is the first razor subscription business aimed specifically at women. FFS supplies thousands of replacement razors every month that attach to their very own (even engraved) FFS metal razor handles, and has just released its first of many additional beauty products – starting with the FFS cationic shave cream.

How has the entrepreneur changed how he thinks and acts in order to create special?
Starting FFS was Aidan's first step into entrepreneurship. He was fuelled by ambition and excitement – but there was also the fear of the unknown.

During the past 18 months, I have seen Aidan grow from an inexperienced entrepreneur trying to make his mark to a leader of an impressive exec board and a business with huge growth potential and ambition. These changes have not happened overnight but have taken months of hard work, stepping outside of his comfort zone, and bouncing back from adversity.

The first significant event came in the December of 2015. Aidan had built an infrastructure and a product – what was missing was the customers. During one of our enablement sessions it was pointed out that very few products were in the hands of customers outside of Aidan's social circles, but it was the simplest of questions that followed which would cause a significant change: *Why?*

The conversation that followed was not one of excuses or denial but about the fear of failure, and the impact it was having on Aidan's actions. The reaction Aidan was feeling is perfectly normal and typical of an entrepreneur; I have seen it many times during the enablement process. The question provided Aidan the opportunity to stop and reflect, and hearing his own voice and understanding his actions created a trigger that led to change.

During the following months, Aidan went on to successfully raise funds with a crowdfunding campaign. These funds would generate a marketing budget that would see his client base rise to over 7,000 subscribers and attract the interest of senior talent.

The next significant event came from rejection. Aidan had grown his customer numbers, his senior team and had made some great connections with partners, but what the business needed to scale was cash. Aidan set off on the investment trail, putting together a well-constructed investment and pitching to numerous VCs. One of which expressed an interest.

Both sides (FFS and the VC) felt that this was a good fit and were excited by the prospects of working with each other. Everything was going to plan. Then over the course of one weekend everything changed.

During due diligence, the VC found articles about the downfall of Aidan's political career, which was sufficient for the VC to withdraw its offer. This left Aidan questioning his position as CEO of FFS, and whether he should step down and let someone else take the helm. Aidan was experiencing a low point on the entrepreneurial rollercoaster. He had invested so much time and emotion into the business – to then be told he was a problem led to him doubting his abilities and ambitions.

During enablement, we would discuss what he had accomplished and whether the opinion of one VC would really reflect that of the entire investor landscape. Like most of us when knocked back, the experience predisposed Adrian to catastrophise. He had assumed that because this had happened once it would happen repeatedly. His flight or fight response had kicked in – and he chose to run away.

Understanding his reactions, Aidan took it upon himself to find out if other VCs would react the same way to his political background. Three months on, Aidan is in advanced talks with another VC whose opinions on the potential of FFS and its team's ability to execute on a strategy far outweigh Aidan's past.

Conclusion

You will see that you now have a methodology for tackling any problems, issues or challenges (choose your term – and don't be afraid to swap it for something else!) in your life as an entrepreneur. I use this all the time. I help entrepreneurs use it too. On many occasions they feel like throwing in the towel. But by following the process of

Re-imagine, GoDo, Re-shape

their problems do not seem so bad and they continue to make progress. It's what entrepreneurial enablement is all about.

CHAPTER THREE
Focus, Focus,
FOCUS

The tyre wall

Imagine a Formula One driver speeding along at 150 mph. It's raining. The track is slippery. As he sees the next bend ahead, tremendous mental agility is needed to decelerate the car, change through the gears and brake at the right moment. The laws of physics mean that, if the car goes out of kilter, it moves from being a controlled piece of sophisticated machinery churning out telemetry and looking awesome to an extremely expensive, out-of-control missile. If the driver is not focused on the race, in tune with his car and thinking about the corner ahead, it will result in lost time – or worse, a trip into the tyre wall.

Consider what a trip into the tyre wall might mean for you as an entrepreneur. The language is flippant but the consequences can be awful. You can be left picking up the pieces for weeks and months. Do not underestimate the possible damage. If you make bad, unfocused decisions that involve cash, people, customers, investors or suppliers, bosses, legal issues and more, it can come back to haunt you. When your focus gets out of kilter, bad stuff happens.

Keeping fully focused over 72 laps of a racetrack is exhausting. But to win, it is not enough simply to get round. The driver must not be thinking about his dinner or the argument he had with his partner last night. So too with the entrepreneur. Keeping insanely focused on the task, the goals and the vision is what this game is all about.

In this chapter I want to look at exactly how a lack of focus can affect you in your efforts to **CREATE SPECIAL** – and share with you what I and other entrepreneurs do to prevent or overcome this. Keeping focused is not easy. It takes real application. It is very much a conscious act. It has to sit right at the front of your brain. But there are some really simple ways to go about achieving it.

Star Wars creator George Lucas has a great saying about focus:

"Always remember – your focus determines your reality."

He's not wrong. So let's make sure we get it right.

The enemies of focus for entrepreneurs

1. White noise

The first enemy of focus for entrepreneurs is a cheeky little distractor called white noise. When you're an entrepreneur, you will be surrounded by people sharing their opinions. There will be dissenters. There will be naysayers. As Dirty Harry said, "Opinions are like assholes – everybody has one."

If I had listened to all the naysayers as I grew Entrepreneurial Spark into the world's largest free business accelerator, I would have been fragmented and frazzled every day.

The effects of white noise are a bit like suffering from tinnitus. If you have been to a noisy concert or a club or listened too loudly to music through your headphones, you sometimes get a ringing in your ears. It can be distracting while it lasts. Eventually it stops. Tinnitus doesn't. It is a life-changing condition. A tinnitus sufferer must concentrate hard to block out the ringing noise and focus on what people are saying.

Being an entrepreneur is sometimes like being a tinnitus sufferer. You have to learn to deal with the ringing in your ears.

2. Procrastination

I love watching people play roulette in a casino. A busy roulette table with players jostling to get their chips down as the wheel spins to a climax is exciting. The players are gambling in a game of pure chance. There are 36 numbers on a roulette wheel, coloured black and red. There is also the 'number' zero, coloured green. A player can bet on red or black, odd or even numbers, or indeed a combination of numbers. Many players have their favourites. Some play safe with their stakes, some go mad.

Either way it's exhilarating to watch – and on a busy table someone often wins big, since so many numbers end up covered with bundles of chips. When this happens and the croupier pays out stacks of high-value chips, it all looks great... and easy.

So I recently gave it a go.

I joined a casino and duly sat watching players at a roulette table. I then sat down and placed £50 in cash on the table. The croupier changed this to 100 chips at 50p value. I was ready. I felt excited – and a bit nervous.

Then it happened.

It hit me like a steam train. I could not make a decision. I did not know where to bet or which 'strategy' to use.

⚡ Should I play it safe and put £5 on odd or even or red or black?

⚡ Should I bet the two-to-one lines on the high or low numbers?

⚡ Should I just go for it and start placing chips on my favourite lottery numbers?

⚡ Should I follow the other players and place chips on their numbers?

⚡ Or should I do a combination of all of the above?

I was frozen to the spot.

I could not make a decision. I had no focus. I felt a cloak of procrastination enveloping me. It was supposed to be fun – but I did not want to have fun with £50 of my hard-earned cash. I wanted to win or break even. But I had no strategy to do so. (And no form of mentor or help to call upon.) All I could think of doing – was nothing.

The loss of focus on what to do to make progress is a killer. I see many entrepreneurs suffer from bouts of procrastination like this. They muddle along with their chips in front of them. They look like they are going to do something. You check in with them a week later. And they haven't. They are sitting staring at the croupier with all their chips in tact, waiting... procrastinating.

3. Blindsiding

Imagine that, out of nowhere, what you have created is blown away by a new competitor, business model or trend. You are motoring along, creating your new creation – and bang! It gets knocked out of the way.

What now?

This is called being blindsided. And it frustrates the hell out of entrepreneurs. It's an enemy of focus because once it hits, believe me, you'll find it hard as hell to focus – but it's also a frequent result of a lack of focus. Blindsiding happens when you least expect it and are not planning for it. It comes out of nowhere like a tawny owl swooping down in the night.

Let me give you an example of where I was blindsided in my time as an entrepreneur.

ISUPERFAN

I invested in a tech start-up called iSuperfan. I really liked the concept and bought into its potential. But unfortunately that is where my focus lay: on what could happen if our customers did as they were supposed to. My head was spinning with the upside and big money.

iSuperfan was going to be a sports trivia computer game that rewarded the top scorer every month with unique prizes based on their favourite team: lunch with the club's manager, for instance. It was going to be £5 for five plays and we had already signed up a Premiership team.

And just imagine how much money we would make (we all talked about it) if only 5% of the global support base for, say, Manchester United played the game for a couple of months...

Unfortunately, I had lost my focus. I hadn't thoroughly tested and validated the basic idea. I hadn't considered being blindsided.

(There were also issues with other directors and team members. We just did not fit well together. I could write write a book on iSuperfan – it was a toxic four months of my life but I learned loads!)

Enabler alert: **Entrepreneurs learn through 'failure'. They use it to go faster and smarter next time. Failing is simply a learning outcome.**

As a result of not having considered the possibility of being blindsided we were, of course, blindsided. Perhaps most fatally, we had not considered that football supporters rarely took desktop computers (or laptops) to football matches. Sure, they had smartphones – but we had launched on desktop...

We had no clue that being on smartphones was the key to us gaining traction with customers. At iSuperfan we all thought our product was wonderful. No one had the courage to say anything to the contrary because the very concept of us being wrong wasn't even considered.

How to find focus as an entrepreneur

1. Keep a #GoDo list

I have about 15 notebooks that I have filled over the
last five years. They're not diaries. I have my diary
on my iPhone, which tells me where I have to be and who I am
meeting. *My notebooks are full of GoDo lists and mind maps.*

What do I mean by a GoDo list? It's not a glorified post-it note,
like something you might stick on the fridge to remind you to
buy milk. No, a GoDo list is action-oriented: massively action-
oriented.

I know that by getting through it, it will bring about genuinely
significant outcomes for both me and those I am working with.

It's too easy to write a list that just covers stuff that you have on
your plate. Here is an example of what I call a Tramadol list:

⚡ Hit the supermarket – bog roll and oven chips.

⚡ Set a reminder for dog's visit to the vet.

⚡ Meet mum for coffee.

⚡ Buy tickets for Michael McIntyre gig.

⚡ Budget for the week's shopping.

⚡ Plan for meeting with my boss.

⚡ Download loan application from bank.

⚡ Be happy!

There is not enough action in this list. It's too vanilla. The
outcomes are not strong enough.

Here is one of my GoDo lists:

1. Compose and send Mike Crow email – compose the text, the ask and get Mike on board. Really important to get Edinburgh result. Chase in five days for outcome.

2. One new word a week: research meaning of *anodyne* and fully understand it. Start to use it in conversation and in *Scotsman* column to best effect. Check for reaction.

3. Write *Scotsman* column and business piece by tonight. Submit via Duncan for approval. Push out via digital channels on Friday at 7am.

4. Call and double check with Admiral insurance re Laura's car premium. Note for April follow-up.

5. Compose full cottage budget list and set aside extension costs. Switch cash to current account and check.

6. Schedule in two hill walks with Belle – one mid morning/ one afternoon. Take iPhone for photos. Send to Laura and Hannah.

7. Post on LinkedIn, Facebook and Twitter – create special. One post now scheduled in weekly together with announcement note.

8. Create one pager on moonshot and get feedback from Ken. Outcomes on investment and valuation scenarios.

9. Lunch with Lorne: preparation on the ask and what is going on in his world right now. Advise on book launch date and get his commitment to promote internally and externally.

10. Buy avocados and salmon for healthy heart twice a week. Check effects on weight and skin.

You can see that everything I do has to be meaningful and measurable. There is an executable action and I am looking for an outcome. The outcome often involves spurring others to take action, so I get bang for my buck as I involve their energies and expertise. And I do this every day. People sometimes ask how I manage it all – staff, a multi-site hub operation, growing and scaling. Here is the answer: constant focus on my GoDo lists, which keep me 100% focused and making progress.

A good actionable GoDo list will also help you sleep and relax. When you do take time out during the day or at night, your head will not be spinning with stuff and fluff. You will have a grip on what is needed and your life will be action-led, not worry-led.

2. Be obsessive about your task, ruthless about distractions

Another great tool for keeping focused is embracing being obsessed about the right things.

When I started to write this book, I got down 5,000 words on my Mac. I sent them to the publisher, who said, "OK, Jim, keep writing." I knew what I wanted to write and over a few weeks 20,000 words came forth. Then I stopped.

It was time to edit and think hard about the next 20,000. I had put aside huge amounts of time to write and get out everything I wanted. But it was time to focus and dig deeper on making the whole theme of **CREATE SPECIAL** alive and relevant and useful to you.

I was obsessed with keeping you with me and wanting to read the next page, the next chapter. My focus for weeks at a time was filtering, distilling and rewording. It required total focus and persistent attention to detail. Was this tough? You bet. But by making time and space precisely for being obsessive about the book, I was able to zero in for long periods of time to achieve the outcome I wanted.

Sometimes you've just got to go all in.

This also requires being ruthless about distractions. As I alluded to earlier: as an aeroplane flies, the onboard computer keeps it in trim. Essentially, the computer is flying the aircraft, taking care of millisecond adjustments, while making mission-critical movements that you as a passenger hardly even notice. This allows the pilot to focus on his unique tasks.

Like a pilot, you cannot truly focus on one thing that makes all the difference if you are out of trim – if you're trying to do everything else at once. Imagine you are tackling an important task for your business. You have set yourself a target for the morning. Ready, steady, GoDo... But wait, your email is pinging on your phone, so you check it and you see you have a couple of important replies to make. Your Facebook is also whirring away and you see a couple of posts that you want to like or reply to. Added to this, you have not drunk anything in a while and you wonder if you should fetch a glass of water. The doorbell goes and you have to take in a parcel for a neighbour downstairs. And on and on...

All this knocks you out of trim and stymies your focus. You have to cut out the distractions. Lock yourself away in a remote cottage if that's what it takes. Or just shut the door to your study, unplug the internet, put your phone on airplane mode, set an alarm for a few hours' time – and GoDo. Give yourself every opportunity not to be distracted.

3. Know when to down tools

Probably one or two days a month, I am at sixes and sevens. I am out of sorts. I am unproductive and not really of any use to myself or others. My biorhythms are out of sync and things are not coordinating in my brain. When I realise that I am having 'one of those days', I down tools and consciously decide not to crack on with important stuff.

We've all had days like this and some self-help gurus will say that you can shake out of them. I don't think you can – not properly. The best thing you can do is recognise that you should not be flying a plane on a day like that. Relax, meander, flutter. It will pass. You will live to fight another day.

Some of you may be asking, 'What happens when a real pilot is having one of those days?' Well, why do you think there are two in the cockpit? And why do you think there are near misses and bumpy landings and poor cockpit communications? They are only human after all. Thankfully, they have a computer, each other and checklists that mitigate as much human error as possible. You don't: so don't go flying your own jet when all is not well.

4. Imagine the unimaginable

The way to avoid getting blindsided is to always be on – even when in sleep mode. This does not mean that you have to be constantly awake, drinking gallons of coffee and chewing caffeine tablets. It simply means you need to be alive to the dangers out there – the threats that can knock you off course or chew you up.

An awareness that you could be out of business, irrelevant to people or that your ideas could be quickly executed upon by someone else at any time really helps you to focus. Oh yeah – it sharpens the senses.

It's an awareness you can achieve by regularly checking for potential problems – blue-sky thinking where the only thing you're trying to see is possible clouds on the horizon. You've got to imagine the unimaginable.

This exercise sharpens the mind to the potential doomsday scenarios lurking out there. My strong suggestion is that you carry out this exercise weekly for yourself and monthly with your team of advisors, volunteers and colleagues. Rather than scare you, it should buttress your confidence in the way you are heading – because you'll be heading there with your eyes open.

Remember, your fellow entrepreneurs (also reading this book) will be up early in the morning thinking about who or what is going to blindside *them*...

BIRTHSPARKS

Here's an example of an entrepreneur getting it right and avoiding being blindsided. I once worked with a company called Birthsparks. Cass, the CEO, had been a midwife. She had worked out that the natural way for women to give birth was not lying on their backs. So she developed the Cub – an inflatable, versatile, recyclable birthing stool that gave mothers an option in how they gave birth.

Cass is now selling them all around the world. She was totally focused, almost with brutal obsession, on what the product would look and feel like and who her customer was. That was because she knew that dropping the ball on either could easily see her blindsided. It would have been easy to take some shortcuts in manufacturing, but Cass was thinking about the long term and the brand and reputation she wanted to build. She knew that you do not mess about when it comes to childbirth. She also had huge respect for her customers – fellow midwives. Cass knew that laser-like focus on winning their hearts and minds was crucial. She could get blindsided if she did anything else.

I was in awe of her determination and focus. When her board made recommendations about investment, she knew that it would cause her to lose focus. Despite setbacks in her personal life and an initial lack of cash, together with gaping holes in the talent pool where she set up the business, Birthsparks as a company thrives today as a result of Cass's focus. When I spoke to her at certain points on her journey, she had the end game in mind and was not going to get sidetracked by new shiny things. Remember, I talked about being ruthless!

When she felt she was getting out of kilter and becoming fragmented, she would reach out to me and others for a wee pep talk or a blether. This energised her and refocused her on what was important and the decisions she needed to make. She epitomises **focus, focus, focus** and is testament to what can be achieved.

5. Defrag your mind

I'm writing this book on a Mac. I switched to Mac from PC two years ago. I really like it, though I know it isn't for some. My old laptop was driven by Microsoft Windows. It performed well. As most older laptops do, it had an old-fashioned hard disk for storage (not a posh flash-based SSD). What I most loved about my old laptop was the Disk Defragmenter utility.

Computer performance gets worse with use and time. That's particularly true for a computer using a traditional hard disk. As I crammed my hard drive with all sorts of stuff, the disk got bogged down, the computer got slower, and bit by bit the laptop became a real pain to use.

Every now and then my hard disk required some disk defragmentation.

Microsoft provided the tool for this. I'd run the defragmentation program once a week. Initially, the program would do a quick check and tell me my hard drive was, say, 25% fragmented and required a tune up. I'd press go and away it went. The display would advise me that my machine was defragmenting and the percentage-completed graphic would let me know that progress was taking place. Once finished – it depended on a number of factors – it would let me know that my computer was now tuned up and ready to rock 'n' roll. My laptop was focused and ready to **CREATE SPECIAL.**

Are you?

You cannot start a business or run a business when you have no focus. That's why you need – every now and then – to defragment your mind.

Just as my old laptop needed a regular defragmentation, so do we as entrepreneurs. How you achieve this is actually quite a personal thing. There's a whole raft of activities out there that are designed to help you focus and de-clutter. Some people like yoga, others a long brisk walk, some like to listen to music, others appreciate a Scottish malt. However

you choose to defragment is up to you. But it is essential that you do it regularly.

> # Think and act
>
> ⚡ What does focus mean for you?
>
> ⚡ Can you tell when you are unfocused?
>
> ⚡ Can others tell you or flag when they see you becoming unfocused?
>
> ⚡ Can you recall a time when you were fragmented and it led to a bad decision or a poor outcome?
>
> ⚡ What do you do now to refocus?
>
> ⚡ What mechanism can you put in place to ensure you defragment regularly?

Help your people to focus too

It isn't just the entrepreneur at the top of a business that has to have time to defragment and refocus. Now is probably a good time to tell you: you will spend half your life fixing people and tuning them up to peak performance so that they can help you to **CREATE SPECIAL**.

People are hugely important to any entrepreneurial venture. They make it or break it. You have to look after them. Think about it this way: no president has been elected, no football manager has won the league, and no successful entrepreneur has made serious money without surrounding himself with great people.

Think about it as an entrepreneur should. After all, as an entrepreneur you're all about understanding other people: customers, competitors, investors. And your people will naturally have health issues, family issues, relationship issues, boredom issues, pissed-off-at nothing issues, religious issues. The list goes on. They are human beings. And almost every day, something malfunctions and needs resetting. *Everything* in life needs resetting now and then. So help them – and give them the opportunities – to do just that.

Don't forget that you cannot help your people to refocus when you are unfocused.

Top tips from total lobsters

Business
Winbox

Working with companies to build email lists organically and create quality content, analysing it to see how it can be improved.

Owner
Marc Woodland

Top tips

★ "Stay focused – don't get distracted from the activities which are important to achieve your goals."

★ "Build a team to grow faster – a team of specialists, the right people in the right places."

★ "Look to develop yourself – every day. Developing yourself will build your business."

★ "Be patient – but always be taking action. You need to keep doing things towards your goals, but you can't expect things to happen overnight."

CHAPTER FOUR
COMFORTABLY
Uncomfortable

Nervous, sick, ill, scared – and I've hardly started

I speak a lot in front of groups of people – at events at Entrepreneurial Spark, NatWest, KPMG, Dell, TEDx and more. And I love public speaking. I have no issues with getting up on any stage: the bigger the better.

I've always been this way and sometimes wonder if I should have been an actor in another life. "You looking at *me*...?" I love to connect with an audience. An emotional attachment makes any talk much more powerful. One of the techniques I employ is a little nerve-racking for those who have turned up to be entertained. Here's how it goes...

Imagine that you are sitting in the front three rows of an auditorium. It is packed. The energy level is high. There are about 300 people there. You know no one. I come on stage – and the first thing I do is say,

"I'm going to pick someone at random from this audience and I want you to come up here and pitch a one minute pitch to everyone on *you*."

It's such a simple request. But people start shuffling in their seats. Things start to get uncomfortable. I then say,

"OK, here I go. Close your eyes. I'm going to come down among you and tap someone on the shoulder."

I leave the stage. I wait about ten seconds. I can see people gripping their seats, hoping I won't tap them. I can feel the fear in the room. I can see people physically look the other way – even with their eyes closed.

That's when I ask everyone to open their eyes.

I'm back on the stage and I let them know I was only kidding. I'm not getting anyone to come up. I can feel the room relax – heck, I can see it. It is visible. It's amazing to watch. It's amazing to feel. And now the audience has connected with me. Also, it likes me – because I am no longer a threat. Everyone can go back to being comfortable.

I ask people how they felt and many tell me – nervous, sick, ill, scared. The most common reaction: *uncomfortable*. This feeling of being uncomfortable is something that human beings really do not like. It's painful. It's powerful.

In fact, **pain is the arbiter of all human behaviour.**

Give me my balls back

We will do any thing to be pain-free – physically or mentally. Think about it for a second. Sitting in an uncomfortable chair, you will shuffle till you feel more comfortable. All men will avoid getting kicked in the balls. (Trust me on that one, ladies.) And you would not wish to go on a date with someone who repulses you. Seeking comfort is the default setting of mankind.

I once watched a TV programme on the elite forces in the British Army. The instructor was in the gym and was covering off a session on self-defence. I thought that the guys he was instructing didn't look like they needed anyone to tell them how to defend themselves – and they knew it. They had egos to match their biceps.

That was before the instructor walked over and grabbed one of the big fellas by the balls. Immediately the recruit winced. His body seized up to try and ease the pain. The instructor walked a few feet still holding the poor man's crown jewels. The other recruits laughed nervously, obviously relieved that it wasn't them in this pickle. The guy was helpless. He would have done anything to have his balls back. Then the instructor let go. The recruit composed himself as best he could. The instructor said something simple but very powerful:

"Every man wants to go where his balls go!"

I'm totally with him on that one. And it brought home to me how important the notion of pain is – and how we will do anything to prevent it or stop it.

We hate to be uncomfortable. Being too hot on a train leads to people opening windows. Watching something on TV that makes you feel squeamish causes you to switch channel. Knowing you have not walked the dog and it could make a big mess on the carpet any time jolts you into getting the lead on and taking her for a walk.

We hate to be uncomfortable... but **living in a state of discomfort for long periods of time is exactly what entrepreneurs do.**

Enabler alert: **Entrepreneurs embrace pain to make progress in life.**

Comfortably uncomfortable

Entrepreneurs exist in a world of:

⚡ uncertainty

⚡ chaos

⚡ ambiguity

⚡ volatility.

They therefore have to have the mindset of **getting comfortable with being uncomfortable.**

Let's examine these words more closely. It's important to understand what we're dealing with. In the second half of the chapter I'll then cover how to think and act like an entrepreneur to overcome them.

Uncertainty

I know that the sun has risen every morning for millions of years and when it is not around, the moon is out lighting up the planet. I'm pretty certain that this cycle will go on way after I am dead and gone. There's a science to it that comforts me. I can download a weather app and it predicts with certainty when the sun will rise in the city I live in – and when it will disappear over the horizon at night. I know that the sun rises in the East and sets in the West. This helps me position my deck chair in my back garden to get the best of the sun in the morning and enjoy its warm rays in the evening. I don't have to think about it – it just happens and I take it for granted.

Enabler alert: **An entrepreneur knows that you like to be comfortable and will act accordingly...**
to **CREATE SPECIAL** to that end.

This certainty is a comfort. But imagine that the planet did not spin at a fairly consistent speed. Imagine it sped up and slowed down when it felt like it. We could not predict or forecast when the sun would rise or set. Clocks and time would be out of sync. Our comfortable little world would be shattered.

Welcome to the life of an entrepreneur.

I'm not saying that entrepreneurs thrive on it. Far from it. It can be exhausting at times, especially over lengthy periods. What I am saying is that they live with it and manage it. They develop a tolerance for it. They get better at it with time.

Think and act

⚡ How do you manage when you face great uncertainty?

⚡ Can you recognise the pain that period of uncertainty brings?

⚡ Do you recognise any behaviours that manifest themselves in periods of uncertainty?

⚡ Do you have coping mechanisms that you have developed?

⚡ What coping mechanisms could you develop?

⚡ Can people see you trying to cope or do you hide it well?

Chaos

The dictionary definition of chaos is an interesting one.

1. *Complete disorder and confusion.*

2. *The formless matter that is supposed to have existed before the creation of the universe.*

Let's add in some descriptors from the Thesaurus:

1. *Mayhem*

2. *Bedlam*

3. *Pandemonium*

4. *Havoc*

5. *Upheaval*

6. *Hurly-burly*

Every time I hear the word *chaos* I am reminded of the late Heath Ledger when he played the Joker in the movie, *The Dark Knight* (2008).

Ledger's Joker is one of the most sinister characters I have ever come across. You will note, I did not say scary. I've seen scarier. But this character is just so completely unpredictable – and there's something profoundly unsettling about that. As he puts it:

"I'm an agent of chaos."

And in no uncertain terms he goes about disrupting and making people uncomfortable, including old Batman. It is his unpredictability that causes so much chaos. It's exactly what went through my mind as I sat at the roulette table and contemplated placing a bet. There is no predictable outcome there. It's organised chaos. So I froze.

This is the context the entrepreneur operates within. Regardless of what words she places on a business plan, reality will never work out 100% like it.

Imagine you have pitched an idea to your family and friends. You want £20,000 to get your idea started. You have two partners who are developing the idea. They also go to their respective family and friends to get £20,000. Between you, you bring in £60,000. You have committed some words to paper in a short business plan and your close networks have stumped up the cash. It's Friday and all is good as you plan for Monday morning when you get started. Great!

But on Monday morning one of your new business partners announces she is pregnant. She needs that £20,000 to see her through her pregnancy and to buy a flat. Her head is now in a very different space. And your other partner fails to turn up for the meeting. You find out that over the weekend he has taken all of the cash out of the account and is nowhere to be seen. £60,000 is gone!

You have a pregnant partner who has lost all her cash, a crook who has stiffed you both, and your own family to answer to.

Your world is in chaos! Total hurly-burly! Complete bedlam!

Welcome to the world of the entrepreneur.

Chaos reigns supreme in the world of the entrepreneur. So many events conspire to prevent or stymie your progress. Chaos constantly tries to knock you off balance. The entrepreneur lives with this, and of course takes steps to mitigate as much chaos as possible. But, nevertheless, it lurks...

Think and act

⚡ Think of a time when you have experienced chaos in your private life or professional life. How did it feel?

⚡ Do you understand how to act and react in times of chaos?

⚡ Can you improve your response to chaotic events?

⚡ Can you grade levels of chaos that you can cope with?

⚡ How do you operate in a group of people either as a leader or team member during chaotic episodes?

Ambiguity

You will have heard the saying, 'The Law is an ass'. I'm in total agreement with this. The goings on in courtrooms all around the world never cease to amaze me. As you know, I was once a police officer. I arrested and detained countless individuals for many offences and crimes – including theft, armed robbery and sexual assault. A police officer is in effect a gatherer of evidence and a reporter of facts. That's what they told me at police college. What they didn't tell me was that in a courtroom, ambiguity is everywhere.

Ambiguity affects us all. As a policeman you write your report on the 'facts' you observe. By the time you get to court, every witness has a different interpretation of what they saw. And then there are defence lawyers, who will quite rightly use all available tools to get their clients found not guilty. (That's their job.) Everything suddenly starts to look vague... It's as if we are all looking at a chandelier in a grand ballroom. Each of us sees the light hitting it from a different angle. We see what others missed, or see what others saw but from a different perspective. The result can be almost completely different accounts of the same event.

Ambiguity causes gaps in evidence, timings, things that were said, what the weather was like, how many cars were around, what suspects were wearing, and who threw the first punch and from what angle.

Ambiguity is a killer in the world of the entrepreneur. The entrepreneur has to ensure that she takes account of all possible perspectives. She has to check and double check for clarity. And avoid vagueness. Good communication is the key here.

Enabler alert: The entrepreneur will eliminate as much ambiguity as possible by communicating well.

It happens to us all, day in and day out. How many times have you sent a text or an email and it has been misinterpreted? How many times have you received a text or email and misinterpreted it? It leads to confusion and, in a great deal of cases, conflict.

Thank goodness for emoticons, eh?

Think and act

⚡ Have you experienced ambiguity?

⚡ How do you communicate with people? Are you specific?

⚡ Do you have an eye for detail?

⚡ How do you record things? In your memory? Notes?

⚡ How can you negate the effects of ambiguity on your life?

⚡ How systematic can you be in mitigating out ambiguity?

Volatility

In the volatile world we live in, everything can change in a heartbeat. I'll never forget the day I watched live on TV as someone deliberately flew an aeroplane into the second World Trade Center tower in New York. I knew there and then that our world would never be the same again. And it has not been.

There is more volatility locally and globally than ever before. Behaviour, trends, brands and celebrity – everything is ephemeral. The short-lived nature of 'stuff' combined with a fast-paced news agenda as a result of social media means that we are living in unsettled times.

This applies especially to the world of the entrepreneur. She has to manage volatility on a daily basis. The variable nature of an entrepreneurial venture means there are no real constants that the entrepreneur can rely on.

The only known constant is that there will be volatility.

Hence the need to be aware of it, plan for it where possible and to learn to live with it. As the entrepreneur knows only too well, there is nothing more certain than uncertainty. Volatility makes sure of that!

Think and act

⚡ Is there volatility in your life just now?

⚡ How do you cope with episodes of volatility?

⚡ Can you recognise and deal with volatile people?

⚡ Do you understand how volatility causes uncertainty?

⚡ Have you experienced any volatile situations?

⚡ How can you recognise when volatility is affecting you or where you are?

How the entrepreneur overcomes

These things aren't going away any time soon for entrepreneurs. It's part of the life. After all, many entrepreneurs when starting out have to confront something like the below. If they pack in the day job and become an entrepreneur they will have to live a life with:

⚡ no certainty of a paycheque at the end of the month

⚡ no certainty of a home paid off in 15 years to call their own

⚡ no certainty of a career path

⚡ no new car every three years

⚡ no certainty that they can take their girlfriend or boyfriend out for dinner and buy them big presents at birthdays and Christmas

⚡ no certainty that if they get ill their company will look after them

⚡ no certainty that if they break a leg their company medical insurance will kick in

⚡ no certainty that they are building a pension for old age.

The only certainty they are now facing is uncertainty.

But the good news is that uncertainty is certainly not fatal or no new business would ever have got off the ground. Successful entrepreneuring is possible. **An entrepreneur is cognitively comfortable with the notion of risk.** To get to that point, it's all a question of:

1. Building up a tolerance

2. Managing risk

3. A growth mindset.

1. Building up a tolerance

I love seeing early-stage entrepreneurs with little self-belief come into the Entrepreneurial Spark hatcheries. They have an idea, no real business experience and the whole thing looks alien to them. They arrive at their first bootcamp and a huge swathe of them cannot make a one-minute pitch on a one-to-one basis – let alone do it in front of 70 of their new peer group.

But then I catch up with them three months later. And they are up there, front and centre, pitching with confidence. They stand out from the crowd.

What happens to get them there? There is no doubt that focus plays a large part. So does practice, sacrifice and discipline. It's not easy to reel off 120 words in a coordinated, compelling fashion in front of a critical but supportive audience in a strict 60-second time frame. But they do. They have moved way outside their comfort zones.

And how do they feel? Many will still be nervous. **But they have built up a tolerance to it simply by exposing themselves to it and staying exposed.** They are living in the uncomfortable zone. That is what entrepreneurs have to do. And it gets easier the more you do it.

Case study: Comfortably uncomfortable

Business name / Name of entrepreneur
Stormburst / Derry Holt

Business proposition / What does it do? / How does it do it?
Game-inspired software for business.

How has the entrepreneur changed how he thinks and acts in order to create special?

Derry came to us an introverted programmer, keen to make his product but naive about the difference between building a great product and building a great business. He learned from Entrepreneurial Spark that the first thing you have to do as an entrepreneur is speak to your customers. This was the first mindset hurdle for him to overcome.

Every day he was challenged by his enabler to find out a little more from his customers – and that mostly meant rejection after rejection trying to connect with them on LinkedIn or through cold calling.

He was miles outside of his comfort zone but after a while he knew this was what he had to do so he just sucked it up and got on with it. Most people are going to say 'no' when you want to talk to them out of the blue but you will eventually get to one that says 'yes' (and if not then you probably don't have a business!). So he stuck at it and got the results he wanted.

Once he found out there was an interest in what he was doing he thought he could go back into coder mode, his real comfort zone. But he quickly learned that he can't ever take his eye off the business. He had a raft of responsibilities in terms of company legalities and managing the output of his friends that were also working with him on the code. He used enablement to work through the emotions that ran with this, trying to strike an authentic balance between the nice guy he is and the need to ruffle feathers as CEO when he has to.

When the beta was ready he had to switch to full on sales mode again. Knowing he had to upskill here to be more effective, he did what many entrepreneurs fear to do – ask for help. He didn't ask people to do it for him, he asked for ways that he could make himself better, knowing that every entrepreneur needs to be able to sell.

Every trial and installation was beset with issues; system integrations taking forever, hot leads blowing cold, problems with training users, matching up calendars for meetings. Each day brought huge highs and crushing lows with pressure mounting as the cash runway grew ever shorter. There is a time when you have to admit that you've got it wrong and that you have something people just don't want, otherwise you could waste years of your life. Yet though there were days where it felt like that to Derry, other days brought him more evidence of customer interest and his instincts told him the time to stop had not yet come.

So he kept making mistakes and learning every day; refining the pitch, creating the right price plan, targeting the right customers more effectively. Then he started to get customers signing up to free trials. Then they started to convert to paying customers. Then he succeeded in getting £150,000 in investment from an institutional investor who liked his team and his business, offering the money to push their growth hard and to back them with infrastructure support.

His backer gave him the £150,000 to spend in six months, knowing that in that tech sector you have to move fast – go big or go home. If they hit their milestones they will get more backing and can create real value in their business. So now Derry has another set of challenges. He has already brought in a sales team so he no longer has to focus there;

his early-stage grit has brought him the experts he needs in that area. Now his challenge becomes managing his people and the early stages of his organisational culture.

Getting the best out of people is not easy, nor is keeping them from leaving you when you help them become amazing. Yet Derry will approach this with the same mindset that he developed though the challenges he faced to get here: realise and forgive yourself for making mistakes as you grow, learn fast by asking for help and understand that your real challenge is simply to be better today than you were yesterday.

Whether this current product is the big breakthrough for Derry or not doesn't really matter, the biggest impact comes from his commitment to changing his mindset. He can now live a life where he knows he can create his own path.

Here are Derry's top tips:

★ "If you can't do it yourself, ask someone that can. The worst someone can say is no, so just ask!"

★ "I've had to pitch to clients in person, cold call and lead teams, and I do all of these things with as much conviction and self-belief as possible. Without any self-confidence, you're only holding yourself down, so I believe that's a key factor in becoming an entrepreneur."

★ "One quote that stands out for me as an introverted developer is 'Fake it till you make it'. None of us will become miracle-working CEOs in a day, week or year. But week by week I see an improvement in my mindset. So don't be afraid to try something crazy – and be even less afraid of the outcomes."

Case study: Comfortably uncomfortable

Business name / Name of entrepreneur
Music Vine / Lewis Foster and Matt

Business proposition / What does it do? / How does it do it?

An online music licensing platform for video producers and filmmakers, focused on providing a highly curated selection of world-class tracks at an affordable price point. With an automated online system and relatively simple internal procedures, Music Vine is a model that has the potential to scale rapidly given the right marketing efforts.

How has the entrepreneur changed how he thinks and acts in order to create special?

When Lewis first came into our Leeds hatchery, he lacked confidence and ambition. He avoided social situations and his intentions for the business were lifestyle-based. Throughout the enablement process, Lewis has developed significantly as entrepreneurial leader, through challenging and pushing him out of his comfort zone he has developed strong networking skills, is an impactful pitcher, and has grown the confidence to successfully secure investment. He has a clear vision enabling him to develop a business that is credible, backable and investible.

> "One of the most valuable things I gained from enablement was realising the importance of being bold. Having great ideas and a strong skill set is all well and good but the potential to have real impact can be diluted if there's an undercurrent of self-doubt or a lack in confidence."

2. Managing risk

My job title when I started Entrepreneurial Spark was Chief Executive Optimist. I had to be. I was that guy who had left a secure career with pension and car and house payments to start my own business – because I knew that I could. But being optimistic doesn't mean you are blind to risk.

There is risk in everything we do – or don't do. You could lose your job simply by being made redundant. I know lots of guys and gals who have clung on to corporate gigs too long and ended up on the scrap heap at the next big restructuring.

Of course, deciding to leave a secure job and start your own venture is not the same as having a change forced on you through redundancy. There's risk there – and it's risk you've chosen. It's a challenge you've committed yourself to.

Being an optimist does not mean ignoring that risk or being optimistic despite it. It means understanding it and making it tolerable – and being optimistic *because* of that.

An entrepreneur is not reckless but works out how to minimise risk to a tolerable level – a level that is comfortable for her as an entrepreneur. If the risk is too high, an entrepreneur might wait until something changes before she goes for it. You want optimism in spadefuls – but not at any cost. **Because entrepreneurs like to win.**

Becoming an entrepreneur is moving out of your comfort zone. Leaving your job. To do so takes optimism. But also balancing an optimistic outlook and total belief in a project with a few checks and balances: for instance, can you attract other people's trust, cash and skill sets? Pitching your idea to others and actually being able to bring them on board is a key part of testing those ideas – and therefore managing risk. You also have to run your numbers. You have to test, test, test before you launch.

You have to manage risk. (The subject of chapter 6 – entrepreneurial discipline – is particularly helpful here.)

3. A growth mindset

The last piece of the puzzle is having a **growth** mindset instead of a **fixed** mindset.

Entrepreneurs always feel the need to grow. They want to find stuff out, experience new things. Whether you're having to use profit-and-loss spreadsheets for the first time, form a company, register a trademark, learn a new language or attend a cake-baking class, you are growing.

Thinking and acting like an entrepreneur means thinking and acting with a growth mindset. You are choosing to continually stretch yourself. If you do the same things day in day out, you are not challenging yourself. And it is only when you challenge yourself that you make real progress. No one ever made anything special happen sitting in a comfort zone.

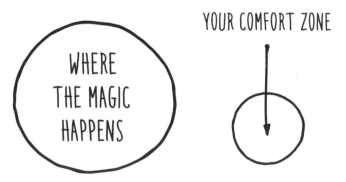

Fixed mindset

Unfortunately, we are conditioned from a very young age to like praise for what we do. *Good boy Jim! You got all your sums right. Well done, Hannah, you got all your spelling correct. Excellent Laura, you scored 10 out of 10 on your vocabulary test.* We loved our parents and teachers praising us. But what this has often done is keep us trapped in a cycle that never pushes us out of our comfort zones.

Praise for doing the same old stuff confines us to a fixed mindset life.

I have worked with many people in life who come to work with a fixed mindset. Life is too hard. They dwell on mistakes. So they carve out things they are very, very good at and stick to them.

One of the worst culprits at producing a fixed mindset in people is our higher education system. Our universities are supposed to be places of innovation. But by teaching students to become experts in just one area, they relegate growth – because there's simply no room for it. It's too easy to think that I am awesome at one subject and not be prepared to go beyond that.

Fixed mindset people suck the energy out of the room and any project that you embark on. They have a negative attitude to change and exploring new ideas. A fixed mindset person is happy to put a great deal of life in the 'too difficult' basket. They believe that intelligence and ability levels are fixed. They will do anything not to grow. They become defensive when challenged. If they are good at one thing, they stick to that. Kings and queens of their own little fiefdoms, they will not budge on anything. It's where they get their confidence.

It is one of the most un-entrepreneurial thought processes on earth and one that you must watch out for in yourself, your friends, family, coworkers, staff and all those around you.

Enabler alert: The entrepreneur enjoys a challenge and accepts it is all part of the game of **CREATING SPECIAL.**

Think and act

⚡ Have you ever been trapped in a fixed mindset?

⚡ Have you wanted to do things you are good at, while ignoring the chance to change or improve elsewhere?

⚡ Do you work with fixed mindset people?

⚡ What qualities or traits do you associate with fixed mindset individuals?

⚡ Is there a fixed mindset trait that runs through your family?

Growth mindset

The constant development of a growth mindset is a wonderful thing. Here is how growth and fixed mindsets differ.

10 GROWTH MINDSET STATEMENTS

What can I say to myself?

INSTEAD OF:	TRY THINKING:
I'm not good at this.	What am I missing?
I'm awesome at this.	I'm on the right track.
I give up.	I'll use some of the strategies we've learned.
This is too hard.	This may take some time and effort.
I can't make this any better.	I can always improve so I'll keep trying.
I just can't do Math.	I'm going to train my brain in Math.
I made a mistake.	Mistakes help me to learn better.
She's so smart. I will never be that smart.	I'm going to figure out how she does it.
It's good enough.	Is it really my best work?
Plan 'A' didn't work.	Good thing the alphabet has more than 25 letters!

A growth mindset is paramount in entrepreneurial thinking. An entrepreneur wants to make forward progress all the time, but accepts that to do so she will have to keep improving as a person.

Waxing – never waning

Let's take a basic example. I am involved with a business that makes candles, wax melts and fragrances. Initially, the entrepreneur in the business simply made wax melts. These are small-shaped pieces of soya wax that sit on top of a burner. Usually a tea-light is inserted into the burner. It heats the wax. A nice fragrance emanates from this and permeates your room.

The entrepreneur in this business was an expert at making melts. They were also her bestseller. Even better, the profit margin on them was very good. So why should she start to make candles? Well, I suggested that despite her current customers liking melts, a whole new trend was opening up in candles. Companies like Jo Malone were making and selling candles from high street shops.

The entrepreneur could have said – No. But she didn't. I was delighted that she did not get stuck in a fixed mindset. It would have been just as easy to choose to do more elaborate melts. To stay in a safe place. Instead she chose growth.

She went away with her pots and pans and experimented in making candles. She tried different wax and oil combinations. She varied the wick lengths and thickness. She tried small jam jar candles and larger three-wick cauldron candles. All the while she was running her business and keeping it afloat selling wax melts. She had many ups and downs as she moved outside her comfort zone. Batches of candles failed. Some set on fire. Some were smoky and some just a bit sad-looking. But she figured it out. She just wanted to get better and better. And she did – until she was able to produce a soya wax candle that burned really well for a quarter of the price of a well-known high street candle made from paraffin wax.

This is what thinking and acting like an entrepreneur is all about – deploying a growth mindset in an uncomfortable situation where the risk is managed to CREATE SPECIAL.

Case study: A growth mindset

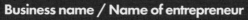

Business name / Name of entrepreneur

Maiden-Voyage.com Ltd / Carolyn Pearson

Business proposition / What does it do? / How does it do it?

Maiden-Voyage.com is an online platform to make business travel safe and sociable for women. It combines recommendations for female-friendly hotels (which have been inspected for compliance) with on-the-ground ambassadors in major cities who can impart local knowledge and recommendations to keep female business travellers safe. It also allows them to find other female business travellers in their location. It also runs female business traveller safety training.

How has the entrepreneur changed how she thinks and acts in order to create special?

Carolyn Pearson is the CEO and has run Maiden-Voyage.com for seven years. She has more than 20 years of experience in a variety of senior IT leadership roles and an MBA with distinction. Carolyn is humbly confident and since the start of her journey with Entrepreneurial Spark has displayed a strong growth mindset. Carolyn was aware of her personal development goals and embraced any opportunity throughout the programme to learn from, collaborate, support and mentor other entrepreneurs.

The enabling sessions were an opportunity for Carolyn to understand herself as an entrepreneurial leader and to give her space and time to formulate her strategy to drive the business forward. Carolyn embodies the spirit of being opportunity hungry. She uses her passion and drive in all that she does and whether she is pitching for funding or promoting her brand she takes every opportunity to leave a lasting impression.

Carolyn remains opportunity hungry and this has been demonstrated in a recent breakthrough which she describes below:

"Three years ago I pitched a semi-formed product to one of the world's biggest banks. There were seven of them and one of me. I remember the meeting distinctly because they ate me for breakfast. I always knew it was a long shot, so I took the feedback with good grace, secretly thrilled that I'd even managed to secure such a meeting.

"Fast-forward two years later, after I had secured investment and I was contacted by one of people who had been at that meeting. She said she had been watching me and Maiden Voyage with interest and was impressed with our growth, news of the investment and our continued penetration into the travel safety sector. She had since been head-hunted by one of Silicon Valley's biggest names and they were looking for services such as ours. At no point did I ever try to sell anything to her, I simply built the relationship, got to understand what they needed and together we explored how we might adapt our services to meet their organisation and culture.

"Almost a year down the line, I was invited to Silicon Valley to run a pilot project which went on to become our biggest contract yet. Of course I try not to travel anywhere without teeing up a few extra meetings in the locale so I booked in to see Airbnb whilst I was there. It was an instant cultural fit and within two days of my arriving back in the UK, they asked if they could fly me out to New York to speak at a conference to 80 of my target audience.

"The funny thing is, I had booked that day in my diary to do American sales calls – standing in front of 80 people, owning the stage, beats making a few impersonal calls any day."

Carolyn has completed the programme and values the time she has spent with Entrepreneurial Spark and she has agreed to come back as a community partner to mentor, coach and provide support to other entrepreneurs. What blows me away with Carolyn is that she is constantly selling and pitching and continues to demonstrate her passion and love for the business whatever the size of the prize.

Conclusion

As an entrepreneur, you will operate outside your comfort zone. You will understand and cope with living with chaos and uncertainty. You know that mistakes will be made – but that is how you learn and get better. You recognise the power of your entrepreneurial gut and how to use this as you build up a tolerance for pain in new situations and experiences. You know that a fixed mindset will stifle you and anything you want to do. You are optimistic and look for the opportunities in events. You embrace a growth mindset and encourage it in others.

The next piece of the puzzle is knowing – and conveying – who *you* are!

Top tips from total lobsters

Business

Myroo Skincare

A completely 'free from' natural skincare brand.

Founder and MD

Rachel Dunseath

Top tips

★ "Collaboration is great – working at home is very isolating, so it's good to get out and meet other businesses."

★ "The opportunity to network is invaluable."

CHAPTER FIVE
Who YOU Are

The glue that binds

This chapter is all about your cognitive framework. That sounds a bit dull and psychobabbly, I know. But I promise you it's anything but. In fact, it's the most exciting topic yet, if you ask me. It's the glue that binds together everything we've discussed so far.

So far we've covered the absolute essence of being an entrepreneur; how to be enabled; the importance of focus; and the necessity of being comfortably uncomfortable. Special things come from these lessons. They are how we can start to **CREATE SPECIAL**. Internalising all of them is the key to that.

And internalising – taking things on board the right way – is where this chapter starts. It's a vital skill, a key part of an entrepreneur's cognitive framework. To do that you need to develop a mindset manifesto.

But your cognitive framework is more than this. It's also about who you are, and how you convey that to others. So we'll also look at how to get to know yourself as an entrepreneur. And then how to be the best – and above all the most authentic – *you* that you can be, in order to win investments and attract talent to your business.

Your mindset manifesto

Political parties publish manifestos prior to big elections. A political manifesto sets out what a party will do if it gets into government. Political strategists, consultants (you know what I think about them) and party leaders sit down and work out what they stand for and what policies they intend to implement.

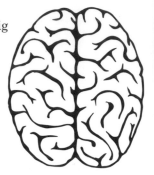

Intend being the operative word. Having listened, polled and consulted voters, a manifesto is published declaring the actions that each respective party will undertake – if given power. The trick to all this is that the tense used is conditional.

A political manifesto is all ifs, buts and maybes. And even if a political party gets into power, things inevitably change as the reality of governing sinks in.

That said, the positive here is that it commits something to paper. A blueprint for action. And it's something that's only produced after having had a good think about things.

Like a political party, *you* have to create your own manifesto as an entrepreneur. But a manifesto unlike any you have seen before.

A different kind of manifesto

We have grown up in an age of self-help. Many people I know sit down with a blank piece of paper and create a plan for the next 12 months: in effect, their own little manifesto. It usually starts with a vision. It will have some goals and objectives. It may go a little like this...

In the next 12 months, I will:

- *run a 10K road race*

- *lose 7 lbs*

- *get promoted in my job*

- *save £5,000 in my ISA*

- *go on holiday to Australia*

- *learn a new language...*

And so on. Some more seasoned manifesto writers will be more specific (especially when it comes to their career). For example...

In the next 12 months, I will:

- *work on my leadership qualities*

- *undertake an executive education course at Babson College*

- *educate myself in entrepreneurial finance*

- *attend a networking event each month*

- *increase my bonus by 10%*

- *improve my communication skills*

- *read three business books.*

This is all pretty standard. There is a focus on external stuff: improving quality of life, body image, money, career and travel. I see these all the time. They state intentions and there is a measure of discipline displayed in actually writing these things down. They are usually done at the start of a New Year. Often they have gone out the window by March. Gym memberships rocket in January and February; by April, it's the same old faces sweating at the machines – the gladiators.

What these manifestos fail to address time and time again is emotional intelligence, emotional well-being and mindset. Why do people never write a **mindset manifesto**?

By the end of this chapter, you will be well on the way to constructing yours. And you will love it – I guarantee. It is paramount that you work on this. Getting a promotion or increasing your pay is really nice, but not taking care of your emotional capabilities and limitations can and does cause all kinds of problems.

Crossed wires

Why write a mindset manifesto? And what goes into it?

It's important to write one because mindset is something most of us get wrong. It's insane how many self-help books are out there. The shelves are packed with them. Why? Well, to be frank, the human race has got pretty damn emotionally messed up. So many of us are only firing on two cylinders right now – because so few people take the time to create (and revisit) a mindset manifesto.

I'm not referring to people with mental health issues. That's a different ball game – and one I know only too well, personally and within my own family. No, I'm referring to a whole slice of humanity that is just not in tune with itself for a number of reasons – but should be.

Here is what a well-wired mindset looks like:

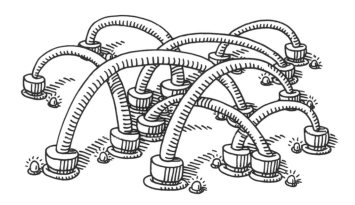

There is order. One thing leads to another. There is structure. Organisation. It has been well put together – and well maintained. This is what it feels like to have solid emotional intelligence. To be able to act and react to life, people and situations while being emotionally transparent with oneself.

Here is what an emotionally challenged mind looks like:

Unfortunately, many of us have a head full of this type of wiring. Coupled with an internal disk drive that is cluttered, the combination is deadly. And it needs sorting out.

With wiring like this there is no system for focus. You can immediately see why this leads to poor performance and a lack of potential being fulfilled.

Think and act

⚡ Do you really know how well you are performing emotionally?

⚡ How can you tell?

⚡ Do you take time to check this each day?

⚡ How do you think your wiring looks just now?

⚡ Do you agree that there are lots of emotionally challenged people out there?

⚡ What do you think is the cause of this?

⚡ Are you ready to tune up your wiring and reorganise your mind?

⚡ Are you willing to be honest now and truly assess how emotionally rounded you are?

Constructing your manifesto

As for what goes into your mindset manifesto, your goals and milestones are things that will be specific to you. Creating your own mindset manifesto is intensely personal. But let me share with you two examples from my life so that you can see what the process involves.

It can seem like a mammoth task – overwhelming when you consider all the aspects of our lives. The key is to be specific and honest. I also like my mindset manifesto to be personal and positive. I suggest focusing on, say, the top two mindsets or thoughts holding you back and work on fixing them first. Then go on from there.

The demon drink

I come from a family full of alcoholics. My father is an alcoholic but I am immensely proud that he has been dry for over 30 years. This is some going. Well done, Jim Snr! But he quite rightly still classifies himself as an alcoholic and abides by the 'one day at a time' philosophy of Alcoholics Anonymous (a great organisation).

I have other family members who are also alcoholics. It would seem that a huge majority of my wider family has a propensity for liking a drink a little too much and a little too often. Indeed one day when I was younger my dad said to me that he thought I would be an alcoholic when I grew up. He saw behaviours in me that were typical alcoholic tendencies. But as a teenager I was obsessed with sport and uninterested in alcohol, so I let it go. I didn't even have my first drink until I was 20.

But the suggestion stuck there in my mind. Especially when I was out drinking with people or at parties. And when I was older, I started to drink heavily. I thought I must be turning into that alcoholic that my dad said I would be. I took some counselling and some time out. I had a really good think about it. Was I my father's son?

Well, when I broke it down, the results were unexpected.

⚡ Did I like a malt whisky? Yes.

⚡ Did I drink to oblivion every night? No.

⚡ Did I drink when I could at every opportunity? No.

⚡ Did I need a drink to get through the day? No.

⚡ Did I wake up thinking about drink? No.

⚡ Did I carry a hip flask or sneak drink into my bag? No.

⚡ When offered a drink when was I able to say no? Yes.

All good so far. But I still liked a malt whisky. So was I disposed to drink – but not actually an alcoholic. How had I been driven to despair? How I had come to assume I was an alcoholic and there was no escaping it?

The things people say to you can have a real (and often unintended) impact – if you let them. I changed my mindset and set my own manifesto on alcohol. Here's how it went:

> "I know that a whole chunk of my DNA is predisposed to alcohol. It's rife within my family. But not me. I don't fall down drunk. I don't pass out. I don't drink whenever I can. I am not an alcoholic, nor will I ever allow anyone to label me as such.

> "If I do drink, it will be my favourite malt whisky. I will not have a single drop before 7.30 pm and I will not have a single drop after 10.30 pm. If I cannot ever get to bed, fall down drunk, fall asleep on the couch with the TV on or have a mental blackout then I will stop and go to AA."

First among equals

Throughout my life, I have always wanted to be number one – the top dog, the big cheese, the head honcho.

A lot of this is about control. You will recall that entrepreneurs like to be in the driving seat. But I remember being the same at school. I loved being in the top ten or coming first in an exam. I enjoyed the feeling of the teacher reading out the exam marks and my name was right up there. Even in the police, I won the academic prize at police college. I guess I studied not to get smarter but to be recognised as number one.

When I started Entrepreneurial Spark, I was front and centre. I knew what I wanted to achieve – and I picked my fights. This was all part of the disruptive nature of Entrepreneurial Spark in its first few years. But there was a bit of ego involved for me as well. I didn't want to hog the spotlight in the Scottish entrepreneurial ecosystem – but I did want to be recognised for holding it to account. I would openly criticise those at the top of the tree. I felt and still do feel that they were protecting their own kingdoms and it was more about them and their organisations than the people they were there to serve. I locked horns with them and was happy to play the 'first among equals' game. Sometimes doing this is not too clever – though it has its place in making change happen.

When Entrepreneurial Spark went ballistic and Royal Bank of Scotland powered it to become a huge scaling organisation, I could have continued to become even more prominent and widely recognised in my role as a champion for entrepreneurs. But I was very conscious of what people call the 'messiah syndrome'

– and I again took some time out to recalibrate and write a mindset manifesto. I took a leaf out of Simon Synek's book, *Start With Why*, and asked myself what I really wanted:

⚡ Did I want to continue to be top dog?

⚡ Was standing on stage and being recognised for this important to me?

⚡ Why did I start Entrepreneurial Spark and was this still relevant now?

⚡ Would my 'first among equals' approach work on a bigger scale?

⚡ What was the right thing to do for the business?

⚡ How would staying or going affect me as an individual?

I decided right there and then to quit. I wrote a new mindset manifesto:

> *"Having created something special that others appreciate, it is time for this entity to fly of its own accord. It no longer needs me to fuel it. The momentum is there. So it's time for me to walk the dog for a bit. I am no longer interested in being first among equals here. I'll help if asked."*

This new mindset of taking a back seat, walking the dog and letting a new CEO create a new legacy took a bit of time to get used to. But it totally feels like the right thing to do. The wiring in my head feels like it is in nice neat rows. My new equal is my puppy – Belle.

These are just two examples of creating a mindset manifesto. They are more than just decisions you choose to make. They are changes in the neocortical part of the brain that work on the limbic part of the brain to help you truly change how you are – and how you engage with life.

Give it a go!

Top tips from total lobsters

Business
5 Squirrels

Helping clinicians launch their own brand of skincare products and mineral makeup.

Founding director
Gary Conroy

Top tips

★ "Keep at it – things will be tough at the start but you have to take the ups and downs."

★ "Write a decent plan and stick to the timelines."

★ "Try and define your business as well as you can."

★ "Don't be surprised when things start to happen. Just because you've had one win, don't think there won't be more."

Who do you think you are?

There is one thing I am really good at and that is reading people. I look right into their eyes and I make an intuitive judgement. Sometimes this judgement can be quite stark, pretty binary – I either like you or I don't.

I throw people a wee tester or a mini curveball. I ask a hard question. How they react to this tells me a lot.

When I am dealing with early-stage entrepreneurs who start to give me a load of old blah blah blah, I stop them dead in their tracks. I ask them how much money they have made this week. That usually does the trick. It refocuses them.

Some get a little pissed off. It's a curveball. They prefer to talk more generally, about stuff that doesn't really matter. This is designed to throw me off the scent. Naughty entrepreneurs! (I usually get an email later that day thanking me for making them face reality – they're not a bad bunch!)

I'm now going to throw you a curveball. See how you react.

As with unsuspecting audiences at the talks I give, I am going to challenge you to really think about who you are.

So – *who are you?*

Write down 100–120 words that describe you. Imagine you have to pitch this in 60 seconds to me. At the end of it, I should know exactly who you are and what makes you tick. Write this down in your notebook or on your smartphone. Spend a few minutes on it.

Think and act

⚡ What did you find easy about this exercise?

⚡ Did you find any parts of it difficult? Why?

⚡ Would you be happy pitching this version of you to a new partner, friend or colleague?

⚡ Does this capture the essence of who you are?

⚡ Would others you know well agree with this?

⚡ Have you been 100% honest with yourself?

⚡ Has this shown up anything you like or dislike about yourself?

It's an interesting exercise. I wonder how hard you thought about it? How far back in your history did you go? Did you delve into your pastimes, likes or dislikes?

When I do this with entrepreneurs who enter the Entrepreneurial Spark hatcheries on day one, I usually get a list of:

⚡ names

⚡ friends

⚡ pastimes

⚡ schools, colleges or universities

⚡ favourite sports

⚡ cars driven

⚡ where they live

⚡ what they like to eat

⚡ marriage status

⚡ kids' names

⚡ and on it goes.

I didn't know myself

In the spirit of sharing, and just so I'm being honest with you, I did a similar exercise five years ago. I thought I knew myself. Here is what I said:

> *My name is Jim Duffy. I am 44 years old and live in Glasgow.*
>
> *I am married and have two daughters, Hannah and Laura.*
>
> *I have run my own businesses and completed a year-long fellowship in the USA.*
>
> *I really enjoy businessy-type things.*
>
> *I have previously been employed at British Airways as a cabin crew member on 747s and spent 11 years in the police.*
>
> *I have a lovely chocolate Doberman called Zeus.*
>
> *I like to run 10K races and enjoy a good Shiraz.*
>
> *My best friend is called Paul.*
>
> *I drive a Jaguar XF 3.0-litre sport, which can go from 0–60 in six seconds. I love my car... In fact, I love cars.*

So, there you go. A 60-second pitch on me from five years ago. You would have known me well at the time, right? When asked to describe Jim Duffy, you would have had a list of stuff to call on. If you had seen me, you could also have added that I was a confident speaker and my dress sense was average. (I used to wear black brogues, black corduroy trousers and self-coloured sweaters from Next – not pretty.)

You would have had a picture in your mind resembling Jim Duffy. But you would not really have known me. *I* did not know me. You had a cursory glimpse into my world. But that is as far as it went. Why? Well, not because I did not want to tell you more. Not because I was being secretive. Not because I didn't put some thought into it.

It was because I didn't really know who Jim Duffy was. I thought I did. I had so many things to say about me. But none of them really got to grips with who I *really* was – and who I really could be.

Five years later, by learning about and taking the time to understand the difference between my **emotional intelligence** (EQ) and my **intelligence quotient** (IQ), I have discovered the real me. It has opened up a whole new world of wisdom. It wasn't easy. I now know why I screwed up so many things and why I can appear moody, petulant, arrogant or aloof at times. Even to those who know me well, who have supported, championed or backed me... And what I can do to be different in future!

For a long time IQ was regarded as the primary arbiter of a person's cleverness. I recall taking IQ tests in school and on entry exams to things like the police. IQ measures intelligence purely in terms of logical abilities. Things like spatial awareness, understanding of mathematics, attention and reasoning. For example: 'What will this shape look like if I rotate it and turn it inside out?' All fairly useless to the majority of us, but pretty cool to the likes of pilots. For decades, kids at school, employees and job applicants were judged on this specific metric. But this has all changed – for the good.

Emotional intelligence has captured the imagination of all who really want to find out how a person ticks, learns, contributes and functions. And while IQ cannot really be improved – indeed, after a score of 115 it makes no real difference to how successful a person is – EQ *can* be improved. And can have awesome results as a consequence.

EQ covers things like self-esteem, intuitive reasoning, empathy, curiosity and social dexterity. These qualities contribute to teamwork, leadership and purpose. And they're finally being taken as seriously as they deserve.

When I was at Babson College, I underwent a whole raft of EQ tests. When I aggregated them and applied what I learned to my past behaviours, it was enlightening. And the amazing thing was that I could spot my frailties – and not simply have to accept them. I could improve my EQ... and so can you. Things like self-awareness, controlling your own emotions, adapting to change and effective listening and communication can all be improved.

Really looking at myself and how I interacted with the world led to a genuine breakthrough. And I still think each day about how others perceive me and how I can leverage my strengths while working on my weaknesses.

So now my answer to the above exercise is quite different. It's not perfect. But I do not want it to be. I am still a work in progress.

> *Enabler alert:* **An entrepreneur accepts that she cannot get perfection and that success is not about being the best. It is about being better than you were yesterday.**

Here is my 60-second pitch now:

Hi, my name is Jim Duffy.

I am an INTJ, which is a Myers–Briggs personality type that suggests I am a visionary. Which is why I hate religion, which is basically someone else's vision – right?

I love being alone. I am an introvert. It is where I get my energy to allow me to **CREATE SPECIAL.**

I detest big mouths; loud crisp-crunchers on trains; bad breath; bullies.

Big groups frighten the life out of me. I like to break them up.

I love to write.

I see things from perspectives others do not.

I get really angry over nothing sometimes; I get fixated on one thing that irritates me. It happens a couple of times a week, when I am really tired. If not checked, I could physically assault whoever has annoyed me.

I cry at the least wee emotional thing on TV.

I don't like funerals or hospitals.

I have a great eye for detail and can read people really well. But I can find it exhausting.

I have a very powerful personality and character that people love: it gets shit done. But I've made some enemies along the way. I regret that.

I am cause-driven. I'm great in bed as I love to give pleasure.

I love a malt whisky and, knowing I come from a family of alcoholics, I make sure – not too much.

And all this has allowed me to build the world's largest people accelerator called Entrepreneurial Spark, where early-stage entrepreneurs are as we speak making huge progress – **CREATING SPECIAL** *– while becoming credible, backable and investable. This makes me extremely proud.*

I have a dog called Belle and I love her.

I'm about to start the third act of my life.

So, there you have it – I'm opening up to you. I can do this because I know who I am and what makes me tick. It's very different from a simple resumé of who my pals are and where I live. I know who I am, what I like and what I am good at. I know where my frailties lie. And how to get the best out of me.

Deep knowledge of yourself allows you to be authentic. To play to your strengths. To work around your shortcomings. To not be too hard on yourself. To get better and better.

How do you get such self-knowledge?

Let's look at one really good way now...

Star Wars and self-knowledge

The original *Star Wars* trilogy is my favourite. I recall going to see the first film as a ten-year-old. I was blown away. I love it when the original trilogy comes on TV, usually at Christmas. I can dream away an afternoon. I am sure you can recall some of the main characters – Darth Vader, Han Solo, Princess Leia, Obi-Wan Kenobi, Chewbacca, the Emperor and of course Luke Skywalker. It wasn't all just spaceships and blasters. Characters as memorable as that can teach us a lot about ourselves as entrepreneurs. I'm serious!

Lots of companies use personality or psychometric testing to assess the suitability of potential employees. When I was selected for the charter class of the Saltire Fellowship, a programme to create and fuel the next generation of business leaders, I was subjected to a barrage of tests. What these tests actually showed was that I was the wrong guy for the programme they were putting together. Nonetheless, I slipped through. Then I went to the USA and Babson College where I was again put through a number of personality and intelligence tests. It's a pretty sterile experience. But I did learn that my Myers–Briggs personality was an INTJ.

That stands for:

I   Introverted

N   INtuitive

T   Thinker

J   Judging

This does not tell you much on its own. Myers–Briggs has 16 personality types. They look like this:

ISTJ	ISFJ	INFJ	INTJ
Responsible, sincere, analytical, reserved, realistic, systematic. Hardworking and trustworthy with sound practical judgement.	Warm, considerate, gentle, responsible, pragmatic, thorough. Devoted caretakers who enjoy being helpful to others.	Idealistic, organised, insightful, dependable, compassionate, gentle. Seek harmony and cooperation, enjoy intellectual stimulation.	Innovative, independent, strategic, logical, reserved, insightful. Driven by their own original ideas to achieve improvements.

ISTP	ISFP	INFP	INTP
Action-oriented, logical, analytical, spontaneous, reserved, independent. Enjoy adventure, skilled at understanding how mechanical things work.	Gentle, sensitive, nurturing, helpful, flexible, realistic. Seek to create a personal environment that is both beautiful and practical.	Sensitive, creative, idealistic, perceptive, caring, loyal. Value inner harmony and personal growth, focus on dreams and possibilities.	Intellectual, logical, precise, reserved, flexible, imaginative. Original thinkers who enjoy speculation and creative problem-solving.

ESTP	ESFP	ENFP	ENTP
Outgoing, realistic, action-oriented, curious, versatile, spontaneous. Pragmatic problem solvers and skillful negotiators.	Playful, enthusiastic, friendly, spontaneous, tactful, flexible. Have strong common sense, enjoy helping people in tangible ways.	Enthusiastic, creative, spontaneous, optimistic, supportive, playful. Value inspiration, enjoy starting new projects, see potential in others.	Inventive, enthusiastic, strategic, enterprising, inquisitive, versatile. Enjoy new ideas and challenges, value inspiration.

ESTJ	ESFJ	ENFJ	ENTJ
Efficient, outgoing, analytical, systematic, dependable, realistic. Like to run the show and get things done in an orderly fashion.	Friendly, outgoing, conscientious, organised, practical. Seek to be helpful and please others, enjoy being active and productive.	Caring, enthusiastic, idealistic, organised, diplomatic, responsible. Skilled communicators who value connection with people.	Strategic, logical, efficient, outgoing, ambitious, independent. Effective organisers of people and long-range planners.

As you can see, I'm sitting in the top right box. The descriptors in the box are accurate. But there is no real context. That is where I feel personality testing falls down. People use it almost as a way of rating themselves – instead of using it to find more ways of enabling themselves.

Enter *Star Wars*. Some clever cookie called GeekinHeals has taken Myers–Briggs and put it in the context of the *Star Wars* movies. Check it out at: **www.geekinheels.com/2013/10/23/ star-wars-mbti-chart**. Can you see which *Star Wars* character being an INTJ makes me?

Woohoo! I'm the mastermind – Palpatine – the Emperor – the Man! The Emperor is an independent mastermind who knows the whole galaxy and has a deep sense of vision. He plots and plans and schemes and thinks. There is a lot going on inside his head and he likes his solitude.

And now I understand more about me and why and how I do things. I am a visionary who gets shit done that really matters and makes people stand up and take notice as I **CREATE SPECIAL**. But I don't like to go to the after party.

Entrepreneurial Spark has nearly 50 staff. And I put all my team through the *Star Wars* Myers–Briggs personality test. It's neither the best nor the worst personality test. There are a ton of them out there. It just works for us.

We currently have a few Darth Vaders, Princess Leias and Yodas. It helps us all work out how we tick. And how we function in the business.

Have a go at a test online. Some are free and some you pay for. Then work out your *Star Wars* character. Have a think about the movies and see where you fit in. Whether you use Myers–Briggs or another personality test makes no difference. The process itself is valuable as it unearths more about you. And don't just accept the results that these tests spit out. Have a growth mindset: you can stretch yourself and change in future.

Once you have had a go at a couple of tests, ask people what they think about you. Tell them you believe you think and act like this or that. They will either confirm it – or set you straight! You can use all of this to gain a better appreciation of yourself and move forward. Taking the time to get to know yourself is important.

An incorrect perception of yourself (or of what others think of you) can lead to many negative outcomes.

Enabler alert: **An entrepreneurial thinker does not live in the past but learns from it and uses it to shape her future.**

Think and act

⚡ If you were to redo your 60-second pitch on you – how would it be different?

⚡ Have you considered how the real you thinks and acts?

⚡ Have there been any situations that you now look back on and understand why things happened as they did, albeit, you never saw them coming?

⚡ At work or at home, will you now be better at getting more positive outcomes as you know more about yourself?

⚡ Test and see if anyone sees any difference in you...

Authenticity

We live in a world where authenticity has never been so important. It's a topic that comes up again and again in business books and articles. It is gathering pace in business schools.

Ten years ago, business schools were hammering out MBAs to keep the lights on while generating the big bucks from *executive education*, which was more or less focused on leadership. Corporate America wrapped itself up in leadership jargon. A new acronym or slogan was born each month.

It got to the stage where it was more or less about branding over content. But over the last few years, content has taken over. It has done so under the banner of **authenticity**. Why? Well, in essence it's what great leadership is all about.

I think the nature of the celebrity-obsessed and social-media-driven world we live in explains why this change has come about.

We live in an age of Kim Kardashian and Kanye West. It's all fake tan and botox. Fake nails. Fake lashes and fake eyebrows. People are inking themselves in the most prominent of places. When I was young, a tattoo was the sign of the working-class man, a sailor or a biker. Women were seldom seen in a tattoo parlour. Now they are their best clients.

We live in the era of the fake Facebook pout. My own daughters update their Facebook image weekly. The outfits may change – the pout never does. But is the pout really them? They certainly don't pout at the dinner table.

This background explains why being authentic is more important and powerful than ever. Surrounded by fakery, authenticity sets you apart. Those of you who get it right will stand out a mile from the crowd.

I meet so many people in my role at Entrepreneurial Spark. Investors, entrepreneurs, consultants, bank staff, economists, mentors, techies, students, professors, accountants, philanthropists... I meet them in many different situations. We have one-to-ones, group meetings, ideation sessions, events, coffees. And what strikes me is how common it is to struggle with authenticity. It's as if there is something missing, something not quite right. Sometimes I feel I'm not getting to the human being underneath the veneer. It can be frustrating. I'm just trying to enable them to move outside their comfort zones. But they hold something back.

Ultimately, that's self-defeating.

If you think about what authentic means, it sets the bar for trust. An authentic piece of jewellery is the real thing, checked by a recognised jeweller and properly valued. An authentic painting hanging in a gallery has the artist's signature on it. It may have a date stamp. It will certainly have been certified by experts as the real deal. These are things we take for granted when we buy a Rolex from a jeweller's or pay to enter a gallery. These are objects that have exceptional value as a result of their authenticity.

> # Think and act
>
> ⚡ What does something being authentic mean to you?
>
> ⚡ Have you seen or bought something where its authenticity is important?
>
> ⚡ Can you see how around you there is a growing culture of inauthentic stuff?
>
> ⚡ How influenced are you by the media, TV, magazines, internet?
>
> ⚡ Does anyone stand out for you as being wholly authentic or inauthentic?
>
> ⚡ Where are your thoughts on why being authentic is crucial whether it be branding or behaviour?

Brand it like Beckham?

I said we'd talk about David Beckham again. I'm bringing him up because he illustrates the importance of authenticity in a really interesting way. He gets it right – but wrong as well.

What sets Beckham apart from us mere mortals is his physique. I take my hat off to him. He is in fabulous shape. As a 49-year-old guy a little on the flabby side, I have huge respect for the discipline it must take to maintain this. I recall visiting New York

City once and seeing a whole building just off Times Square wrapped in a sleeve showing David in nothing but his boxer shorts. It epitomised how the Beckham brand is built: on clean living, fitness and diet.

And it all seems very authentic. After all, the guy is in great shape. So I bought into it as much as anyone. (Though I'm not buying his boxer shorts just yet.)

All was well with brand Beckham for me – right up until I saw him advertise a whisky brand. His own, as it happens. Haig Club.

Folks, David Beckham does not drink whisky. He most certainly does not drink grain whisky. And he does not order huge glassfuls at public bars. Everything about this is wrong.

And on so many levels. Can you imagine what state Beckham would be in if he had two of the large measures he's shown with in promotional pictures? His team would not let him be seen in public.

It's inauthentic. It's a brilliant example of what every entrepreneur should avoid – just as much as what else he does is an example of what you should cultivate. David Beckham has certainly **CREATED SPECIAL**. But endorsing a whisky brand isn't an example of it.

To avoid this kind of mistake and to be truly authentic you need to ensure that you have a solid understanding of who you are and who you are not.

Who are you?

Think about what words you would want others to say about you when asked to describe you. What would they be?

⚡ Would you like people to say you have integrity?

⚡ That you are honest?

⚡ You care for others?

⚡ You are consistent?

⚡ You have strong values?

⚡ You have a solid moral compass?

⚡ You think about others?

⚡ You are a family man?

⚡ You are a terrific mother?

⚡ You are a trusted friend?

⚡ You can be totally relied upon?

⚡ You finish what you start?

⚡ You are authentic?

These qualities say a lot about you. Others that you know or will meet will pick up on these messages and align themselves with you – because of them! And this allows you to **CREATE SPECIAL.**

> *Enabler alert:* **An entrepreneur knows that people buy people. Businesses are built on emotion. He capitalises on this.**

Imagine you have to pitch to an investor. You are asking her to invest £250,000 in your start-up. Yes, two hundred and fifty grand. That sounds a lot. In actual fact it happens month in and month out. So it's a realistic number to pitch for. Investors are comfortable with it. What do you think the first thing is that goes through the investor's head while you make your pitch?

Perhaps:

⚡ Is this good value for money?

⚡ Who is the competition if I invest?

⚡ Who else is investing?

⚡ What equity am I buying?

⚡ What does the business plan say?

It's none of those. They are all fair questions. But the question going through the investor's head is:

Why would I invest this money in YOU?

The first thing an investor always wants to know about is the human being she would be giving her cash to. She will only give it to you if you are credible. If there is any doubt whatsoever about you, she will not invest. Even if the idea is a stonker. If you have not hit the character sweet spot, the investment will not go ahead.

I've seen entrepreneurs get so close to raising investment but fail because the investors just see something in the entrepreneur that worries them. It can be a number of things: economy with the truth, manipulation, playing games, being obstructive or a lack of consistency. Ultimately, it all comes back to authenticity.

To **CREATE SPECIAL**, you have to have an authenticity about you that others can invest in.

If you can capture the essence that is you and improve upon it, you can harness the amazing power of people. They will come to you to help you in your endeavours. It's not about charisma or ebullience. Remember, I am a Myers-Brigg *I* – an Introvert by nature. It's about people having a feeling that you are sincere and will do what you say you will do (with their money!).

Enabler alert: **An entrepreneurial thinker and actor creates confidence in people as they believe he will do what it says on the tin.**

The power of an open book

As you **CREATE SPECIAL** you want and need others around you to help you and believe in you. They are looking for the real deal. Not an imitation of you. They want to see a human being who they can rely upon and will not let them down.

They want to see you naked.

No, not like that!

They want to see you *emotionally* naked: that is, honest.

You have to start living your life not being afraid to be emotionally naked. It's not as bad as it seems. Some of the best entrepreneurs, leaders and influencers of the past century lived their lives this way – Gandhi, Mandela and Martin Luther King to name a few.

They did not have a lot of money and did not set out to be rich and powerful, but look at the impact they had. Being authentic and doing things for the right reasons brings people to your side. Having people by your side is wonderful. Nothing beats human support in anything you do. It beats money hands down. It is the surest way to **CREATE SPECIAL.**

You will hear the expression, "She's an open book". You will also hear the expression, "He's a game player". Open books do really well in this life. By being an open book – not being afraid to show your emotions in a sensible way – people feel more comfortable with you. **With an open book mindset, there is no win or lose – just progress.**

Game players may feel they are winning, but in the long run the game wins and they lose.

By open book I do not mean stupid, naive, raw, unsophisticated or unworldly. Far from it. By open book, I mean you are genuine and honest about yourself with others. That engenders trust. People can see your authenticity – so they are comfortable with your messaging. They do not need to decipher what is going on inside your head or the course of action you are really taking.

By being straightforward, you enkindle trust. This is indispensable.

> *Enabler alert:* An entrepreneurial thinker and actor knows the games are out there, but plays a straight hand to get where she wants to be – and others around her appreciate it.

The war within

As you make progress on getting your thinking right, at times there will be a war within you. The old you and the new you will square up to each other. If you are not careful they will cancel each other out and you will be badly hurt.

There will be times when you are in the zone. It feels great. As if you are at one with yourself and this planet. But, out of the blue, a dark shadow will rise and throw a spanner in the works. It just happens. It's your subconscious trying to get back to a default position, where there is comfort again in a fixed mindset. This war occasionally rages in all of us. You have to recognise it for what it is – human weakness. And that's OK.

Getting to a stage where you know how to be emotionally naked and maintain it is amazing. But people, events and just the way the human mind works will sometimes conspire to tangle everything up. Those are the moments to take time out for a minute, an hour or a day to reorganise your wiring and get back into the zone.

Conclusion

We have looked at you and your wiring, your personality and how important it is that you know and understand it. Taking time every week to have a think about your actions and reactions as they pertain to you and how they impact or influence others is powerful. It cements or destroys relationships. Knowing how to rewire and enable your engine management system to operate at peak performance for long periods of time helps you **CREATE SPECIAL**. When added to your own brand – your own personal brand – this brings resources around you. You have to be the most authentic version of you that you can be. Be you and others will appreciate you for simply being that. And finally, think about the day you have to pitch to that investor – whoever that may be.

CHAPTER SIX
BETTER
Every Day

Entrepreneurial discipline

Now that your cognitive framework is taking shape – organised, honest, authentic – you are ready to take on the world. But to **CREATE SPECIAL**, time and commitment is required.

I see many start off with great intentions. They know where they want to go. But they lack the stamina and skills to execute. Usually, this is because (as discussed earlier) they fail to skill up and continually develop themselves. But in many cases it is because they lack the discipline and fortitude to deliver awesome value over a long period of time. They lack structure. And they fail to grasp that it doesn't matter what everyone else is doing – it only matters that they are getting better bit by bit.

They need **entrepreneurial discipline**.

Think and act

⚡ Have you ever started something with great intentions?

⚡ Did you fully see it through?

⚡ What causes you to give up or not finish something?

⚡ Do you know anyone who is constantly starting things – like diets – and never finishes them?

⚡ As you think about creating special – is there anything in you that worries you about your own self-discipline?

⚡ Is there anyone you admire who has seen something through that inspired you?

⚡ Are you ready to inspire others with your execution attitude?

It's time to add some real discipline and self-direction to who you are and what you do.

Let's consider what I mean by entrepreneurial discipline. I'm going to use three examples to explain it: a high street start-up, a first-century Roman gladiator, and one of the most popular Olympic athletes of the past decade. All have something valuable to teach us about what it takes to be a truly disciplined entrepreneur.

Top tips from total lobsters

Business
Knight Franchises
Finding buyers for franchises.

Managing director
Adrian Knight

Top tips

★ "Take on a client or two and perfect your systems, then scale up."

★ "Validate your business model as a priority – and keep going through that loop until it is validated."

★ "Ask for help, ask for support – keep asking."

A soapy start-up

Starting any business is not something that should be taken lightly. When starting a business, most people have that 'aha' or epiphany moment when they suddenly realise that they want to change something or do something better. I have countless examples of people coming to pitch their million-dollar idea! They then go online and have a wee look at the subject area. But they do this through rose-tinted glasses. They then speak to family and friends, who (with some honourable exceptions) tell them exactly what they want to hear. They remain wholly optimistic. Their excitement is palpable.

It goes something like this:

"I'm going to open a soap shop in the high street and people will flock to it as they buy

lovely new soap. I'll be so happy selling my soap and chatting to my lovely customers. The shop will smell wonderful and the colours and hues will be inviting. I just can't wait to open my business and dive right in. Everyone will want to visit my shop. I need to get a website. I need to get on Facebook. I'm going have so much fun getting a name for my new business."

This is typical of many retail types who, over a glass of wine, cook up a whole new life for themselves. This is undisciplined behaviour that ends up costing people a small fortune. It's a messed up way to start any business. And this is why thousands of shops open up and close down within 12 months all over high streets the length and breadth of Britain.

So just in case you are thinking of doing this – don't!

People always want to take the easy route. Remember, we don't like pain. So we will live pain-free if we can. It's easy to listen to the happy bunny voice in your head rather than the vicious little bastard on your shoulder who asks the tough, uncompromising questions based on the rules of the game.

And there *are* rules to being a successful entrepreneur. If an entrepreneur does not follow some of them, she is doomed. The rules are there to keep you in check so that you get better at whatever you do. Let's look at the soap shop against the background of entrepreneurial discipline. Here is what a disciplined approach would look like:

⚡ Who is my customer?

⚡ Who is buying soap these days?

⚡ How do they buy soap? Online or in a supermarket or in smaller shops?

⚡ Would people pay a premium for my soap?

⚡ Where would I open my first shop?

⚡ Should I even open a shop?

⚡ What business model works best? A subscription box?

⚡ Should I do a pop-up shop?

⚡ What do I know about trends in soap?

⚡ Do I need any qualifications or dermatological experience?

⚡ Where will I make my soap?

⚡ How much can I make?

⚡ How many other one-off 'mom and pop' soap shops are out there?

⚡ What can I learn from them?

⚡ When can I visit them?

⚡ Is anyone investing in soap shops?

⚡ What are the top five new soap products launched in the last 12 months?

⚡ Where will I advertise my soap?

⚡ How much does it cost to acquire one of these customers?

⚡ How much does it cost to keep them as a customer?

⚡ What is the lifetime value of one of my customers?

⚡ How do I show my soap is special and demonstrably different?

⚡ Where can I test if people will like my soap?

⚡ How do I validate this with 100 people?

⚡ What insights might this give me?

This list could go on for another 25 pages...

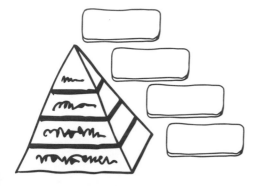

𝒯𝑜𝑝 𝑡𝑖𝑝𝑠 from total lobsters

Business
AMPLYFI

Software developer of platform that identifies and tracks new and emerging trends, potential technology advances and highlights sources of possible market disruption.

CEO
Chris Ganje

Top tips

★ "The most valuable resource that you have is your time. Get to 'Yes' or 'No' as quickly as possible with potential customers, suppliers, investors, and then move on."

★ "Most start-ups fail because they fail to execute. Be ruthlessly honest with yourself about your idea's value proposition. If it shows promise, do not hang about congratulating yourself."

> ★ "If you truly believe in your idea, never give up despite what the world around you might be telling you."

Starting a business with entrepreneurial discipline at its heart is really hard. Indeed painful. It's enough to put you off starting at times. But it is this discipline of dealing with all the hard questions and vagaries of business that takes you to where you ultimately want to go: a successful business, **CREATING SPECIAL** in the world.

The true entrepreneur knows there's a way to go before she takes the keys to her soap shop on a three-year fully insuring and repairing lease. She has to know that she is getting better in her subject area every day. By doing so she has a better chance of survival when she makes the leap.

You can see how strongly I feel about entrepreneurial discipline in a new business. By constantly asking questions that test you and your business idea, you and your idea get better.

> *Enabler alert:* An entrepreneur will constantly question her understanding of a subject to ensure she becomes an 'anorak' and can answer any questions on it. But, she doesn't stop there...

There is structure in this stage of thinking and researching. If conducted well, it leads to better execution. *Execution* is a word that is making all the red carpet appearances in executive education, entrepreneurship books, pitch decks, TED talks and online blogs. Why? Well, it really matters. It is the difference between life and death in a business. Strong, well-informed and well-researched execution is critical if you want your business to still be going in 12 months' time.

YOU are Spartacus

As I write this book, Kirk Douglas, the well-known American actor, is turning 100. He is now a centurion. But boy he still looks fit. His son, Michael, is also a miracle of modern science: he is in his 70s and looks like he could outrun and outgun me still.

Kirk Douglas starred in many movies over the years. One in particular has special meaning for the entrepreneur. It's a real epic – *Spartacus* (1960).

In the movie, Douglas plays a rebellious slave, Spartacus, who is sentenced to fight as a Roman gladiator. Spartacus does the unthinkable and leads a gladiator revolt – escaping slavery and fighting off the Roman Empire until the odds finally overwhelm him and he his caught, along with his fellow ex-slaves, after eventually losing a battle. You'll no doubt remember the scene where they all refuse to identify Spartacus. It keeps the Romans from singling him out for punishment. "I'm Spartacus!" "*I'm* Spartacus!" "*I'm* Spartacus!" (They are all executed.)

Recently, a multi-episode version of *Spartacus* was made for TV. It is brilliant and captures the true essence of what it means to be a gladiator. It captures the true essence of what it takes to be an *entrepreneur*. (Don't worry: getting crucified by the Roman Empire is not part of it.)

With the luxury of multiple episodes to unfold its tale, this version of the Spartacus story is able to dwell on an important trait required in a successful gladiator.

This is also the trait that you require to **CREATE SPECIAL**. Many people are not willing to knuckle down to this. But though it sounds hard, knuckles aren't actually involved! It's definitely not as brutal as joining a ludus or gladiator training school. In fact, you'll enjoy it.

It's all about learning outcomes. And learning to love them.

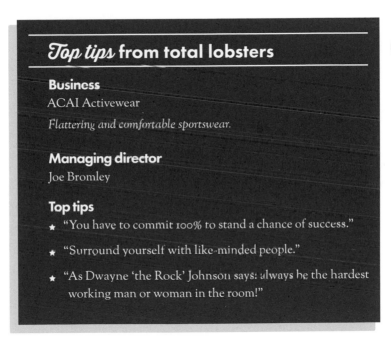

Top tips from total lobsters

Business
ACAI Activewear

Flattering and comfortable sportswear.

Managing director
Joe Bromley

Top tips
- ★ "You have to commit 100% to stand a chance of success."
- ★ "Surround yourself with like-minded people."
- ★ "As Dwayne 'the Rock' Johnson says: always be the hardest working man or woman in the room!"

Learn to love learning outcomes

Getting up early and practising all day as a gladiator was tough. By practising, I mean fighting and skilling up with weapons like swords. A gladiator had to learn not just how to fight and win. He also had to learn how to lose. Or rather, to learn *from* losing.

Every single encounter in the ludus (or gladiator school) had to imprint upon the gladiator's mind a *learning outcome*. Instead of simply going through the day and getting by – fighting and practising – the gladiator broke down each intervention into specific chunks. He then pin-pointed lessons from winning and losing within those chunks. He replayed them in his mind. He worked out why he won or lost – so that he never got caught out by a move again.

Using the knowledge of each encounter every day built up a mindset so disciplined it was effectively pre-programmed. His instincts became stronger than ever. He took nothing for granted. He had to innovate in every sparring session – using what he had already learned. Even when tired or having a bad day or not really in the mood, the gladiator could not slip back into bad practices.

If he got sloppy and undisciplined, this would lead to a beating – and a lack of respect from his peers. Sure, he wanted the accolade of winning in the arena. It was the pinnacle for a gladiator. But to get there took months of iterating on learned behaviours, building upon technique after technique. These techniques became imprinted upon the gladiator's sub-conscious, emblazoned in his muscle memory. He could perform them in his sleep: he just got better and better and better.

This is the discipline that you need to **CREATE SPECIAL**. Trust me, it's not hard. It's not hard at all. It just takes time and patience.

Enabler alert: An entrepreneur aims to be the best version of herself that she can be at any given time.

Sometimes we go through life passively learning things about ourselves and others, science, history, anything else that comes across our radar... We soak it in. But we don't think about it. And what goes in one ear very often goes out the other before we know it. But if you think of all new knowledge and experiences as things with **defined learning outcome**s, you start to store knowledge in a way that pays off. You learn and grow dramatically.

Let's have a think about how you can respond proactively to what you learn and experience as an entrepreneur. It will enhance your discipline. It will mean getting constantly better at what you do.

I want you to try something this week. Over the next seven days, take part in the seven-day gladiator challenge. I know, I know. It sounds like one of those infomercials or TV adverts on dieting. *"Lose 7 lbs in seven days or your money back."* (Of course you're going to lose 7 lbs when you spend seven days eating nothing but celery.)

But there's nothing nonsensical or lightweight about the life of an entrepreneur-gladiator.

The seven-day gladiator challenge

MORNING RITUAL

1. Set your alarm an hour earlier.

2. Have a book by your bed. Get out of bed and read a few pages. If you have a loved one in the room, go some place else so as

not to disturb them or be disturbed. The book can be fiction or nonfiction. Think and reflect.

3. Now check the temperature of your emotions. How do you feel this morning? Anything bothering you? Write it down in order to clear your mind. Make sure you have no clutter that could impede you doing battle.

4. Think about the day ahead. Family, friends or work. Write down anything you feel you want to accomplish.

5. Select two outcomes that you will work on for the day. Write them down.

6. Leave the house with a clear mind, ready to do battle in whatever comes up.

DURING YOUR DAY

1. Treat everyone you meet as hostile. I don't mean be nasty to them. Simply view them as having a big sword that can hurt you. They are ready and willing to attack. So be alert and alive to what could happen. Think about how you would counter and defend should they attack. Remember, they also are gladiators. And none of them want to lose.

2. Treat every interaction – every conversation and meeting – as an opportunity to learn about yourself and improve. Listen carefully to what your opponents are saying. Don't view the moments when you aren't speaking as merely periods when you are waiting to speak. Actively listen. Afterwards, consider: did you get the best out of each situation? If you approached a situation a different way, could you have got a better outcome? Have you left any encounter feeling frustrated? Have you failed to see off another gladiator?

3. Are people aware of you? Do they know that you are now in gladiator school and are working not only to survive – but to get constantly better. Can they see you have raised your game?

EVENING RITUAL

1. Did you make progress on the two outcomes you wanted to achieve? What small progress did you make? Have you iterated on one thing to get closer to getting it over the line?

2. What did you learn from dealing with your 'opponents' today? Did you get blindsided? Did you manage your emotions well to make progress? What barriers stopped you? Do you feel that someone or some situation got the better of you – and you got a sword in the guts?

3. Were there conversations or situations where you saw a threat or a challenge? Did you use your defensive tactics or sword effectively? What did you learn about these encounters that you can use again? How can you improve your instincts with this knowledge?

4. Write down how you feel and what you will take into tomorrow.

5. Clear your mind and think about your body and mind as a lean, mean, fighting machine that is getting better. Go to sleep knowing you gave of your best and have lived and learned so that you can fight another day.

Spartacus had to start somewhere. He could not be the Champion of Capua overnight. It would take months – and a right few television episodes – before that happened. So I'm not expecting you to be the Champion of Capua overnight either. You have to be willing to get better at a pace that may at times frustrate you.

Entrepreneurial discipline is not acquired in the blink of an eye. It's a medium to long-term synthesis of experience with reflection and resolution. It's about learning about yourself and situations in life – and building on that.

With this new discipline comes a better ability and capacity to **CREATE SPECIAL**. Rome wasn't built in a day. Neither was a great company like Apple. It took applied thought and action and constant learning to become awesome.

You can do this. It will change your life.

I spent some time in the police service, as you know. It is a disciplined service. Orders are given and followed. But at no point did I feel that I was getting better each day. I did not feel that I was progressing into a better-rounded and more capable individual, becoming even more of an asset to my colleagues or my community. Far from it. If I look at the fitness regime, for example, it just did not make sense. In the first two years of my training – the probationary period – I did indeed have to keep fit and regularly underwent fitness tests every three to six months. But after this period I never actually had to engage in any planned or scheduled physical activity as part of my role.

That is why we had so many roly-poly cops out there, who ended up with hypertension and heart conditions way ahead of their time. Out of what was a 30-year career (now 40 years as pension rules have changed), I only had to be physically disciplined for two years. Go figure!

We were, in theory, a disciplined organisation. But we had no physical discipline. We actually promoted a *lack* of discipline. The staple diet on the back shift was fish and chips, doner kebabs and curry.

Not so for the gladiator in the ludus in Capua. If a gladiator does not perform and get better, he will take a hiding. Taking a beating in the ludus is all fine and well. Wooden swords were used for training purposes.

But being beaten in the arena in front of the screaming crowds? That meant certain death.

Sporting inspiration

Mo Farah vs Justin Gatlin

In the UK, everybody loves Mo Farah. That beaming smile he has when he crosses the finishing line – it inspires many of us to be better.

Farah has taken years of training to get to where he is. He is a clean athlete. By this I mean he has never taken performance-enhancing drugs. All his victories are built on hard work, discipline and an attitude of getting better and better in small training breakthroughs. He epitomises what I mean by the gladiatorial approach to being better than you were yesterday. He grinds out small but meaningful wins and learns all the time about his body and how to be a better runner.

Contrast this with Justin Gatlin. Gatlin is an American 100-metre sprinter. Like all sprinters he has the strong physique that is needed to produce explosive power to hurtle him forward at speed. Gatlin has also worked hard at his sport. But he decided to circumvent the rules to get success more quickly without going through the correct gladiatorial steps. In short – he cheated.

Gatlin served two bans for taking prohibited substances. Some argue that he should never have been allowed back into the sport. But he is still running and competing today.

Why am I highlighting both these athletes? Well, ask yourself this – which of the two **CREATED SPECIAL**?

Creating special needs discipline in whatever you do. Trying to take shortcuts or get there in a different way does not work. In fact, it impedes you.

> *Enabler alert:* An entrepreneur knows that everything takes twice as long as it is first imagined.

Becoming an Olympic athlete like Mo Farah and winning regularly at that level is an extreme example. He is a one in a million. But the way he has done it reinforces the power of **CREATING SPECIAL**. It's not just the gold medal at the end at any cost. It's the whole journey: the getting up at the crack of dawn every morning to train. Eating correctly, a strict regimen of exercise, stretching and moulding your body and mind into what it takes to succeed. Iterating and improving. Making lots of small breakthroughs over a long period of time.

> *Enabler alert:* An entrepreneurial thinker and actor competes with themselves to improve – not with the competition.

Top tips from total lobsters

Business

The Futsal Partnership

Franchisor of firm coaching children based on the modern coaching principles of Futsal.

Group managing director

Matt Goodman

Top tips

★ "Get out and talk to people – networking is so important and you never know where things will lead."

★ "Look after your cash – my previous business expanded and borrowed in the wrong way. Cash is just so important!"

★ "Never give up."

No re-sits

As you create special you build upon the successes and failures that you experience day in and day out. Treat every success and failure as a learning opportunity and the lessons become programmed into your memory. And you get better and better.

I once knew a respected entrepreneur. Sure, he was a millionaire, in fact a multi-millionaire. He had a pretty decent team and life was good. He was making investments, as many seasoned entrepreneurs do. He knew retail pretty well. But he started to get greedy. He was enticed into the world of London commercial property. Before 2008, this market was booming and there were big gains to be made: gains that were totally illogical. And, as we now know, were unsustainable and built upon pure greed. But they all seemed like sure things! As you played the property roulette wheel, it always came up with a win.

The entrepreneur became deeply involved in this market. He borrowed more and more to buy more and more. Entrepreneurs like to use other people's money; this guy used a big UK bank to help fund his roulette investing. This, of course, left him a bit exposed – despite all the gladiatorial battles he had been through, which had taught him to watch his flank for danger. He had the scars from previous battles in the arena over a well-documented and successful history as an entrepreneur. Now he was down in the sand without a sword, with two big hairy gladiators bearing down on him. But he was too distracted by greed to act.

Then it came...

The 2008 property crash and global recession was devastating for him and many others. Despite all his years of gladiator training, he came unstuck. And it was painful. He had been blindsided and it was too late to react. He was badly injured.

Luckily it was not a fatal blow. But he had to be carried out of the arena. It was not what he was used to.

He had got down to his last £20 million. Of course, that doesn't sound too bad, does it? But given that he once had £500 million, you can imagine the pain.

Like all good entrepreneurs, he refocused. As a true gladiator does, he regrouped. He put all his efforts back into his training. He became a master again with his sword. He scaled down the private jets and got the train. This time remembering all he had learned. He re-shaped his team. His mantra is now:

NO RE-SITS!!!

Imagine if you worked on his team now! You'd make sure that every *i* was dotted and every *t* was crossed. He has built fellow gladiators in his image. They have his back as he enters the arena. They are Spartacus too. This is what the best entrepreneurial gladiators do.

This entrepreneur is once again the Champion of Capua – and I have huge respect for him. He is back to treating every encounter as a learning opportunity, every day as a day in the arena. He has true grit.

Grit

Grit is the last component of discipline. I want to test and boost your grit. Grit is one these onomatopoeic words that feels as it sounds. The gutsy, snarling feel that the word has is a great place to start in understanding what it means when it comes to **CREATING SPECIAL.**

Because it is all about guts. Let me give you an example.

Between 2 April and 14 June 1982, the United Kingdom was involved in a ten-week war with Argentina. This was called the Falklands War. Argentina invaded and occupied the Falkland Islands, claiming sovereignty over them. During the conflict, 255 British military personnel died, with 649 Argentinian deaths. Three Falkland Islanders also died during the war. The British prime minister at that time, Margaret Thatcher, was a gritty, determined lady. No one was taking the Falklands under her watch. Britain sent an armada of ships and sailors and fighting troops – the Task Force – thousands of miles south to regain the islands.

The geography of the islands, the distance to travel there from the UK, and the weather all made recapturing the islands a logistical nightmare. One truly amazing snapshot of behaviour stands out for me. It is grit personified.

British Royal Marines and members of the British Parachute Regiment disembarked from ships at San Carlos on East Falkland on 21 May 1982. They then had to walk (or, as they called it, *yomp*) some 56 miles in full battle gear carrying weapons and ammunition. They did this in three days, carrying 80 lbs of equipment over rugged, freezing terrain. The ground was mostly peat bog or jagged rock. The average wind speed was 19 mph. Rain and sleet soaked them through. They had no tents. Tents would have been too heavy. They just had ponchos to keep warm.

The state of the British kit was not all that good, either. The soldiers' boots leaked and many of them developed trench foot, together with blisters and sprained ankles. You're probably beginning to see how tough this yomp must have been. But hold on...

This was simply them going to fight!

This was not the actual battle. After the uncomfortable travel in heavy seas down through the Atlantic to the Falklands, they had to march all that way in those conditions.

Then they had to go into battle...

And they won!

I find this grit absolutely awe-inspiring: total steely determination to power through and achieve an objective. It makes the hairs on the back of my neck stand up.

I want you to put yourself into their shoes for a few moments. Imagine you are six miles into this yomp. You are freezing. Your feet and hands are numb with cold. The wind is cutting into your face. The weight of the kit you are carrying is feeling heavier with every step over uneven ground. One wrong step, any lapse of concentration, and you can go over on your ankle. It's dark and bleak and you can't just say, "Screw this, I'm going home!"

No, you have another 50 miles to go. You cannot let your colleagues down despite the feelings of dread and isolation and cold.

Overcoming all of this over 72 hours is what grit looks like.

With grit, anything is possible. A human being can accomplish amazing things. Grit is what gives you the strength to overcome obstacles and see things through to the end. It allows you to get better by keeping you in the game no matter what.

> *Enabler alert:* **An entrepreneurial actor who has grit at her core can trump anyone with talent but without grit.**

True grit is what makes entrepreneurs stand out. If it was all about talent, many more successful entrepreneurs per capita would be produced around the world. Talent gets you only so far. When the chips are down, it takes more than talent in your field to get the deal over the line or create that version of special that matters to you. It takes more than being clever to **CREATE SPECIAL**. I see lots of talented people wither on the vine. They do not possess grit.

Similarly, if it was all down to luck, many more entrepreneurs would be successful. I know lots of lucky people who are just not taking it home to mama.

A gritty personality that never gives up, that lives way beyond what is comfortable for many of us in a world of ambiguity and danger, is what makes the difference. It's the last piece of the gladiatorial entrepreneur.

Top tips from total lobsters

Business
Senergy Innovations
Developing a polymer plastic solar thermal panel that is cheaper, easier to install and aesthetically improved.

CEO
Christine Boyle

Top tips
* ★ "Perseverance – you just have to keep pushing for small wins."

* ★ "Patience – you're not going to be high flying in a few months."

* ★ "Partners – you can't do it on your own. I've learned that working with universities and consultants."

* ★ "When you're listening to people all the time you can expect them to have all the answers, but it's really your call. You've got to have your own answers."

Conclusion

Is entrepreneurial discipline painful? Are there sacrifices? Of course. But I think being only half-committed causes you more pain. It leads to disappointment not just for you, but for those who follow you and believe in you. Having a 'no re-sits' mindset as you power through each day and the challenges it brings you results in a winning mentality. And, funnily enough, in winning.

Thinking about and acting upon learning outcomes as you win and lose, pass and fail, all helps to shape the gladiator you are. Remember, unfit police officers are no use when it comes to chasing bad guys. You have to be ready to yomp at a moment's notice.

Now, let's see how all this toughness in attitude and winning through mentality helps you as you create special in your moonshot.

Enabler alert: An entrepreneurial thinker and actor faces the world with a steeliness that is unshakable.

CHAPTER SEVEN

Your

MOON

SHOT

Under the moon of love

This is our last chapter together. So let's raise the bar even higher for each other. It's what you expect now that you are a gladiator. I want to leave you with a different kind of feeling when you think about **CREATING SPECIAL** for you... Let's start with some questions:

Think and act

⚡ What do you think about when you look at the moon?

⚡ What is the moon?

⚡ Do you know how far away it is in miles? Have a guess?

⚡ Can you imagine what it is like up there?

⚡ If you were offered the once-in-a-lifetime opportunity to go there for a day – would you?

The moon is pretty awesome. Unlike the sun – a huge burning ball of gas that radiates a colossal amount of heat and energy – the moon has no power source. It has nothing that burns and nothing that produces any heat or light.

It just hangs there. But its glow has always enchanted mankind. There is something special about the way it shines on a dark night.

2016 saw a gorgeous super moon, when it was the closest it had been to the earth for 70 years. It was 14% bigger and 30% brighter than normal. But even when it's normal, it's inspiring and more than just a teensy bit magical. No wonder we talk of the man in the moon. Lovers meeting in the moonlight. Strange things happening at full moon. Things that happen once in a blue moon.

And the all-important (and all-too-rare) action of **shooting for the moon**.

Now that you're all empowered as an entrepreneur, you didn't think you'd be doing something unexceptional did you? No, now it's time for your **moonshot**.

Moonshot thinking

Apart from his tragic death, I remember President John F. Kennedy for three things:

⚡ The Cuban Missile Crisis, where he showed some big balls and faced down the Soviet Union. That was a close one!

⚡ His 'friendship' with Marilyn Monroe. Norma Jean was quite a lady – and you know what they say about politics, power and celebrity.

⚡ His vision for putting a man on the moon.

Think about that last one for a second. *Putting a man on the moon.* If you don't think about it, it doesn't sound that hard. Just pop him up there and it's job done. I would guess that when JFK stated his intention to put a man on the moon, many didn't realise the gargantuan size of the task ahead.

It was 25 May 1961 when Kennedy set out his vision. The USA was head to head with the Soviet Union on a number of fronts. The competitive tension between these two superpowers created good things and bad things. Only a few months earlier, the Soviet Union had put cosmonaut Yuri Gagarin into space. This made him the first human in space. The Soviet Union gained bragging rights across the globe. *Check us out, comrades – we have a guy in space and you don't!* This mightily embarrassed the USA. And as we have seen it do throughout history, it reacted.

The USA does not like to be beaten at anything. JFK's announcement had political overtones. There was an 'Anything you can do, we can do better' feel to it. Well, that's America for you! America now contemplated landing a man on the moon before the decade closed. It had to shoot for the moon.

Once the president had set out his vision for the ultimate moonshot, it was up to others to make it happen. Imagine the excitement. A massive budget was available. Huge resources were put into it. *Make it happen!* And they did. But to do so they had to think bigger: much, much bigger.

To make their moonshot, they had to adopt **moonshot thinking**.

Moonshot thinking is not about moving the dial just a small turn. A small turn is not enough. It is about ripping the dial out and replacing it with a new one: it is ten-times improvement – not ten per cent gain.

A gain of ten per cent is all fine and well if you want to improve your score on a test or your time in a half marathon. But ten-times improvement is what was needed to catapult an enormous payload into space and dunk it on the moon. Not to mention bring it back safely with everyone alive... The astrophysical calculations alone would have been mind-boggling.

Because mankind did this almost 50 years ago we take it for granted. It was 'business as usual'. When you truly consider the scope of what the USA and its scientists and astronauts did – it is breathtaking.

Your own moonshot

Now it's your turn.

It's time to think hard about creating your own moonshot. It can be something really simple or really complex. That is up to you. *A moonshot is something of significance to you.*

𝒯𝑜𝑝 𝑡𝑖𝑝𝑠 from total lobsters

Business
Pillow
Helping holiday home owners left behind by the digital revolution.

CEO
Scott Weir

Top tips
* ★ "Don't accept bad clients – be very selective about who you work with, especially when starting out."

* ★ "Systematise your business as soon as possible – everything that is replicated should have a system in place."

* ★ "Have faith in yourself – a lot of people will tell you that you can't do it, you have to believe that there's something inside you that can."

The main components of moonshot thinking are:

⚡ scaling your thinking

⚡ being unreasonable.

Scaling your thinking

When I created Entrepreneurial Spark, I started small, with some volunteers and a few guinea pigs who wanted to create their own special. But, even as a small, insignificant start-up, I acted so much bigger than I was.

I talked bigger and thought bigger. I had a go at organisations and people that were a lot bigger than me. Not from a position of arrogance but from a position of *insurgency* – trying to be a visionary for what could be.

Sure, there were times when I was bloody frustrated. People would try and hold me back. A few I had upset plotted behind the scenes with those who had supported me to do just that. But what we were delivering was hitting a sweet spot. Our mindset was different. It was the key to moving the dial. *Before we scaled the business up, we scaled up our thinking.*

When I talk to early-stage entrepreneurs, I always urge them to scale their thinking first. Consider it this way. Making a paper aeroplane is doable. It's a simple piece of origami. To go from that to making a NASA rocket requires – before anything else – a mindset shift.

Many lack the ambition to scale their thinking. It takes real effort. There's a degree of defying gravity at first. And you have to really think things through. A moonshot mindshift is hard. It takes you places that will be uncomfortable. But that's where the magic happens.

Case study: Scaling your thinking

Business name / Name of entrepreneur
Whisky Frames / Kristen Hunter

Business Proposition / What does it do? / How does it do it?
Rustic photo frames made from whisky barrels.

How has the entrepreneur changed how she thinks and acts in order to create special?
Kristen came to her interview to join the Entrepreneurial Spark hub with her husband Ross. We could see that

Kristen lacked confidence in her abilities as an entrepreneur, however her nervousness just demonstrated how much she wanted the opportunity. We loved the product, it was unique and they could answer the obvious concerns we had around the supply of whisky barrels.

As soon as Kristen joined she made an effort to attend all the elements of the programme from pitch practice to workshops, as well as being physically in the hub and taking the time to get to know her fellow entrepreneurs. She wasn't someone who loved pitching but she powered through, building her confidence and an engaging pitch that impressed her fellow entrepreneurs and mentors. At our first meeting I challenged Kristen on admitting areas she was less keen to explore, essentially this was around financials and in particular knowing her COGS (cost of goods sold). At this point Kristen's ambitions were to supply distillery gift shops around Scotland but through setting bigger goals she quickly understood that the opportunities were there if she decided to go for them, and she did.

I've witnessed Kristen go from someone who thought she had a business that might add to the family income, transform into a competent, positive, proactive entrepreneur – and she did all of this while having her second daughter, Louise.

Recent good news has included gaining a further 80 new stockists, with potential for an additional 50. Exporting to Australia, Gibraltar, USA, Malta, Germany, France and Korea. Winning 'best product' at Scotland's trade fair. A large department store in Sydney placing a big initial order. A major retailer wanting a trial pack of 300 of each frame for their USA stores as well as further distilleries, museums and international distributors getting in touch.

An early breakthrough came after a recommendation by a fellow entrepreneur to attend a specialist gift trade show. Kristen attended and gained more than 40 stockists, including some very prestigious names. This early success gave Kristen the realisation that the sky really was the limit. She put in place plans to increase production of frames and identified what equipment, staff and processes she'd need. Following a win of £3,000 at the bank sponsors awards, new wood-cutting equipment was purchased and two full-time staff were employed.

But perhaps the thing that blows me away most is that Kristen attended events despite being heavily pregnant (overdue in fact). Kristen and her husband Ross also tag-teamed baby care so that they could attend the full day of Acceler8. That's impressive dedication!

Being unreasonable

I want you to be unreasonable. I want you to promise me you will be as unreasonable as hell in some things.

Sometimes this is so easy for me. My *Star Wars* character, the Emperor, is driven by his own ideas to seek improvement in stuff. I always ask hard questions. I love to start with *Why* – and keep asking it. There is an old tool out there that still has much relevance today. It's called the **five whys?** You ask *why* for a number of times until you get to the bottom of things. Asking things like "Why is that?" or "Why did that happen?" helps you unearth meaning. It increases your knowledge.

Yes, it really does help to be unreasonable. Not belligerent or rude – just unreasonable in that you want to get to the nub of things so that you can make improvements.

Steve Jobs was unreasonable. He demanded first class, world class and the best from his leadership team and employees at Apple. They knew that. That's why many of them worked there. 'Mediocrity' and 'middle of the road' did not feature in his vocabulary or psyche. His unreasonableness ensured Apple became number one and disrupted so many other business models and industries. It was his sharp elbows that hustled and sparked Apple to greatness.

People are often happy to whitewash this with a vague fairytale of innovation and genius, a focus on the products and services Apple sold... but *he* made it happen... and we need more like him. We need people like you to be a bit more Jobs-like.

Case study: Being unreasonable

Business name / Name of Entrepreneur
ROVCO / Brian Allen

Business Proposition / What does it do? / How does it do it?
ROVCO is a Remotely Operated underwater Vehicle (ROV) service delivery and subsea inspection company. Its unique offering is the ability to create perfectly scaled, three-dimensional graphical maps and models of subsea infrastructure – a service sought by the offshore renewables, oil and gas industries. This replaces the current method of subsea survey using video. The firm believes that as its technology gets adopted it will be disrupting a $1bn industry and will be able to create a business worth nearly £100m within five years.

How has the entrepreneur changed how he thinks and acts in order to create special?
Brian is a fantastic example of an entrepreneur who came in with one idea before being challenged to scale, grow and accelerate through enablement. Rising to the challenge, Brian changed his approach and entrepreneurial mindset, pivoting and accelerating in a new direction. On

application, Brian was aiming to grow his business to a turnover of £2 million within the first five years. After a short period of enablement, ROVCO found itself through to stage three of a tender contract worth £21 million. While unsuccessful on that occasion, it opened Brian's eyes to what was possible for ROVCO.

In Brian's own words:

> "When I first joined Entrepreneurial Spark I had a business idea to start an ROV business running vessel and harbour surveys around the country and an aim to grow to having a c.£2m turnover within five years. After going through the enablement process I realised that this was maybe an easy growth plan rather than true acceleration and I started to try to find ways that I could achieve more – we went international in three months with one ROV working out in Fiji and two on a project in Oman.

> "The real change came from moving from a mindset of 'What can I build?' (and keep control of) to one of 'What's the best that could be built with all available resources?'. I went from being a control-focused entrepreneur to a wealth/acceleration mindset. Once I opened myself to the opportunity of bringing in investment, I started to look at what would be needed to attract an investor. What could I do with the additional resources and what's the best that I could create?

> "Instead of self-limiting I started to look at opportunities that would come along, and instead of turning them down for being out of reach or too risky, I started to work backwards and work out how best they could be achieved. What individual steps would need to be taken to de-risk it and achieve success?

> "Once I started to work like this I quickly realised that almost anything is possible. This was never more true than this very week – when we were asked to tender on a £40,000 difficult dry dock survey involving six

different techniques in a very short space of time. Initially it looked so hard, complicated and risky that it was better to turn it down. However, after working through all the issues and how to de-risk it we're now tendering and expecting to win."

Brian is a humble, hardworking, gifted entrepreneur who refuses to take his current position for granted. Despite being a naturally talented entrepreneur, the thing I love about Brian is that alongside his passion, dedication, talent and aptitude he still has a drive and ambition to continue learning from others and developing his own skill set. Brian understands the importance of surrounding himself with 'people that know more than he currently knows' and I personally believe that this trait will see his success eclipse that of some of those that have mentored him along the way. This apprentice entrepreneur is likely to become a master...

My moonshot

This book has hopefully given you new ways of thinking about yourself, your emotions, your focus and how you skill yourself up. The whole point of it is to make you realise your ability to **CREATE SPECIAL** in a way that only you can.

To **CREATE SPECIAL** brings awesome value for you in this life and the lives of others as they follow you, support you or benefit from what you create. It's time to hold your breath and reach for the moon.

I'm actually being selfish here. As we come to the end of this book, **I want a return on my investment as well as a return on your investment.**

> **𝒮nabler alert:** An entrepreneurial thinker and actor always has several plates spinning at the same time to ensure multiple positive outcomes.

Imagine if thousands of people throughout the word have had a bloody good go at creating their own moonshot as a result of reading this book over the next few years. The world will be a far better place. Many of you will not just have **CREATED SPECIAL** but will be recognised for it by your family, friends, coworkers, members of parliament, charities, corporates and more.

You don't know it yet, but you are *my* moonshot. I'm counting on you to #GoDo – and then one day look me up and tell me all about it. That's if I don't read about you online or in a newspaper first!

Complete the following sentences:

My name is _____ and I'm going to **CREATE SPECIAL**.

My moonshot will _____ .

Enabler alert: **An entrepreneurial thinker and actor knows what it means to take your breath away...**

Conclusion

There are only a handful of people who can say that they have walked on the moon. I am not one of them – yet. This number is dwindling, as we no longer put people on the moon. That's a shame but it's encouraging that some people are actually aiming for Mars these days... One day, a human being will step foot on that planet. And Mars is about 35 million miles away. The moon is 238,900 miles away.

How about you? Do fancy being that person who sets foot on Mars?

I'm getting older. As I do so, I look at all the missed opportunities that I blew over the years. I don't regret them. I can just spot them now that I'm (supposedly) a bit wiser. One thing I do know is that I only have one shot at this life. I'm living my moonshot right now. And so must you.

Enabler alert: **An entrepreneurial thinker and actor does not ask for permission, he asks for forgiveness later on.**

I want you to use everything we have gone through in this book to achieve your own moonshot and **CREATE SPECIAL**. We live in a world of chaos. Entrepreneurs act through pain. They don't ask for permission and they keep getting better. They are gladiators. Just look at people like Elon Musk, as he becomes the new NASA with his SpaceX company. He's just a man, right? He's not a god or an extraterrestrial. People like him push the boundaries and scale their thinking to be more than they should be. They are living their lives to the full.

Whatever age you are. Whatever stage in life you are at. Whatever resources you have at your disposal. You can **CREATE SPECIAL** now. You can think and act like an entrepreneur now. You know their secret sauce. The genie is out of the bottle and it's now up to you to #GoDo and make some magic.

CONCLUSION

You only get one life. It's something that terrifies me and excites me at the same time. I hope it terrifies and excites you too.

I have one final mental exercise for you.

Imagine you are now 80 years of age. You are living in a care home. You are lucky and have family that visit and bring you gifts on your birthday and at Christmas. Your sight is failing and your hearing is not as good as it should be. You wear a hearing aid. You cannot make out the characters on the TV and you need someone to tell you the time. You have false teeth. You sit at dinnertime with 50 other 70–80-year-olds. You all eat soup and drink tea. Your digestion is not what it used to be, so no fillet steaks and triple-cooked dripping chips with a bottle of Malbec to wash it all down. You can only just manage to wipe your own arse when you visit the loo. Sometimes, you need help. You take a concoction of pills each morning and at night to stave off diabetes, raised blood pressure and the pain from your hip. You sometimes wake up during the night disoriented and afraid. You think you are in your own house, then realise you are not. You regularly forget the names of the carers and nurses. You're not sure who you know in the care home as people come and go... and die. And all you have are your memories...

That is the time for you to remember what an awesome life you led and how you **CREATED SPECIAL** for yourself and others.

Top tips from total lobsters

Business
Mobile Pay Systems

Developer of a showcase point-of-sale till system called SWOPOS that integrates cash, card, contactless and mobile payment methods, and pre-order payments. It also links into a business's accounts and marketing.

CEO
Lee Nazari

Top tips

★ "Know what your strengths are – and let go of your pride and understand that if someone is better than you at a certain part of the business you don't like, then get out the way and let them have the freedom to shine. You might even be impressed."

★ "Stay mentally positive. Really cultivate a strong mental state. It's the fuel for your drive, and if you're not positive you can't drive the business forward."

★ "You've got to believe in what you are doing – it's a cliché, but you can't do things because somebody else thinks it's good or because it might make you money. Choose your path for the right reasons: doing something you don't enjoy is no way to go through life, you are then just existing. We are not here to just exist, we are here to live."

That's the memory I want for you. Live your life as if there was no tomorrow and be the best version of yourself that you can be. Make sure you are firing on all four cylinders as much as possible. Be authentic and people will believe in you. Be honest when you make mistakes. Think big. Be disciplined. Skill up in life and not on a soulless, one-dimensional CV. Show true grit as you act and react to what takes place. Be prepared to get sore feet as you yomp 56 miles in full battle dress. Focus like a Formula One driver as you take each bend in the pouring rain. Don't get blindsided and hit the tyre wall. Wake an hour early. This is your hour to prepare for the day. Make time to tune up your internal hard drive and defrag it so it is whirring away at optimal performance.

Good luck to you as you create your own moonshot memories. Please let me know how you get on... If you do, you will be a big part of my moonshot as I sit in that care home with wonderful memories of all that you have created.

THANKS
FOR READING!

Our readers mean everything to us at Harriman House. As a special thank-you for buying this book let us help you save as much as possible on your next read:

(1)

If you've never ordered from us before, get £5 off your first order at **harriman-house.com** with this code: cs5t

Already a customer? Get £5 off an order of £25 or more with this code: cs525to

(2)

Get 7 days' FREE access to hundreds of our books at **volow.co** – simply head over and sign up.

Thanks again!
from the team at

 Harriman House

Codes can only be used once per customer and order. T&Cs apply.